Walk in God's Pattern for Success

JOHN BEVERE

Charisma
HOUSE
Books about Spirit-Led Living

ꙅThe Inner Strength Seriesꙅ
LIVING WITH STRENGTH IN TODAY'S WORLD

WALK IN GOD'S PATTERN FOR SUCCESS by John Bevere
Published by Charisma House
A part of Strang Communications Company
600 Rinehart Road
Lake Mary, Florida 32746
www.charismahouse.com

Unless otherwise noted, all Scripture quotations are from the
New King James Version of the Bible. Copyright © 1979, 1980,
1982 by Thomas Nelson, Inc., publishers. Used by permission.

Scripture quotations marked KJV are from the King James
Version of the Bible.

Scripture quotations marked NIV are from the Holy Bible,
New International Version. Copyright © 1973, 1978, 1984,
International Bible Society. Used by permission.

Scripture quotations marked NLT are from the Holy Bible, New
Living Translation, copyright © 1996. Used by permission of
Tyndale House Publishers, Inc., Wheaton, IL 60189. All rights
reserved.

Cover design by Ka.. .l Campbell

Library of Congress Catalog Card Number: 2001098131
International Standard Book Number: 0-88419-837-5

02 03 04 05 87654321
Printed in the United States of America

Contents

Introduction

From the first moments of Creation, God established a pattern of divine order on earth that would usher in the glory of God—and assure man, His finest created beings, of fulfillment and success in life.

What Is Man?

When I consider your heavens, the work of your fingers, the moon and the stars, which you have set in place, what is man that you are mindful of him, the son of man that you care for him?

—PSALM 8:3–4, NIV

I believe, though I cannot prove this, that Psalm 8 records the response at Creation of one of the mighty seraphim angels that surround the throne of God. Stop and think of this, and try to see through this angel's eyes. This awesome, mighty God, who has just created the universe and put the stars in place with His fingers, now comes to a little speck of a planet called earth and makes what appears to be a tiny insignificant speck of dust into the body of a man.

> From the first moments of Creation, God established a pattern of divine order on earth that would usher in the glory of God.

But what really amazes this angel is God's total focus of attention. It's fixed entirely on this being called man. We are told by the psalmist that His thoughts toward us are precious, and that the sum of them is so great that if they were counted, it would be more than the sand on the earth (Ps. 139:17–18). In seeing this, I believe this angel cries out, "What is this that You are so interested in and fondly affectionate toward? What is that little thing that is constantly on Your mind—the total focus of Your plans?"

Take the time, be still and consider the works of His hands. We are told to do this. As you do, Creation will preach a sermon to you. It will declare His glory!

As you read this book, it is my sincere prayer that you will understand God's pattern for success found only through following His divine order for life.

Adapted from John Bevere, *The Fear of the Lord* (Lake Mary, FL: Charisma House, 1997), 29–30.

ONE

Divine Order Brings God's Glory

DEVELOPING
Inner Strength

God spent six days bringing divine order to the earth. Then He brought order into man's body. Once divine order was achieved, God "breathed into his nostrils the breath of life; and man became a living being" (Gen. 2:7). God literally breathed His Spirit into this human body.

Man was created in the image and likeness of God, and then woman was taken from the side of man. Neither had clothing or a covering. "And they were both naked, the man and his wife, and were not ashamed" (v. 25). All other creatures were given coverings. Animals have fur; birds have feathers; fish have scales or shells. But man did not need an outer covering, for the psalmist tells us God "crowned him with glory and honor" (Ps. 8:5). The Hebrew word for "crowned" is *atar*. It means "to encircle or surround." In essence, the man and woman were clothed with the glory of the Lord and didn't need natural clothing.

The blessings this first couple experienced were indescribable. The garden yielded its strength without having to cultivate it. The animals were in harmony with the man. There were no sicknesses, diseases or poverty. But best of all, this couple had the privilege of walking with God in His glory!

It was the first night of four scheduled meetings in Saskatchewan, Canada. The pastor was in the process of introducing me, and I would be on the platform in just under three minutes. Suddenly, the Spirit of God began to walk me quickly through the Bible, revealing a pattern occurring throughout the Old and New Testaments. The pattern is this:

1. Divine order
2. God's glory
3. Judgment

Before God manifests His glory, there must be divine order. Once His glory is revealed, there is great blessing. But also once His glory is revealed, any irreverence, disorder or disobedience is met with immediate judgment.

God had opened my eyes to this pattern in less than two minutes, and He let me know I was to preach it to the hungry congregation of Canadians before me. That evening was one of the most powerful services I had held, and I want to share its truth with you.

From the Beginning

To lay a foundation, let's go to the beginning. When God created the heavens and earth:

> The earth was without form, and void; and darkness was on the face of the deep. And the Spirit of God was hovering over the face of the waters.
>
> —Genesis 1:2

The English words "without form" are a combination of the two Hebrew words *hayah* and *tohuw*. Together these two words render a more descriptive account: "The earth became formless and chaotic." There was no order—just *disorder*.

Though the Spirit of God hovered or brooded over this chaos, He would not move upon it until the Word of God was released. With God's spoken words, divine order was set into operation on this planet. God prepared the earth for six days before He released His glory into it. He took special care with the garden He had planted for His own. Then God created His man—the focus of creation.

Once the garden was prepared, God "formed man of the dust of the ground." Science has found every chemical element of the human body resident in the earth's crust. God designed both an engineering and a scientific wonder.

Judgment

God first brought divine order by His Word and Spirit. Then His glory was revealed. Blessing abounded, but then came the Fall. The Lord God commanded the man not to eat of the fruit of the tree of the knowledge of good and evil, for to disobey would be immediate spiritual death.

> With God's spoken words, divine order was set into operation on this planet.

Mocking God, Satan challenged God's Word with his twisted contradiction, "You will not surely die. For God knows that in the day you eat of it your eyes will be opened, and you will be like God, knowing good and evil" (Gen. 3:4–5). Then Adam, with full knowledge of his actions, chose to disobey God. His irreverence was nothing less than high treason. When this happened, judgment followed.

At once Adam and Eve knew they were naked. The glory had departed, leaving them uncovered and separated from God in a state of spiritual death. In a futile attempt to cover their nakedness, they hastily prepared a few leaves and vines and clothed themselves by the work of their hands. God saw what they had done, pronounced judgment upon them and clothed them in tunics of skins. Most likely these skins were from a lamb, foreshadowing the Lamb of God who would come and restore man's relationship with God. Then the fallen couple was driven from the garden where eternal life was found. Judgment was severe—the result of Adam's irreverent disobedience in the presence of God's glory.

The Tabernacle of His Glory

Several hundred years pass, and God finally finds a friend in Abram. God makes a covenant of promise with Abram and changes his name to *Abraham*. Through this man's obedience, the promises of God are once again secured for generations to come. Abraham's descendants end up in

Egypt as slaves for more than four hundred years. In their hardship God raises up a prophet and deliverer named Moses.

Once the descendants of Abraham are delivered out of bondage, God brings them into the wilderness. It is in the wilderness of Mount Sinai that God outlines His plan to dwell with His people. God tells Moses, "I am the Lord their God, who brought them up out of the land of Egypt, that I may dwell among them" (Exod. 29:46).

Once again God will walk with man, for this has always been His desire. Yet because of man's fallen state, God cannot dwell within him. So He instructs Moses, "Let them make Me a sanctuary, that I may dwell among them" (Exod. 25:8). This sanctuary was called the tabernacle.

Before God's glory comes, there first must be divine order. Therefore, God carefully instructs Moses how to build the tabernacle. He is very specific on all points of who is to build it and who is to serve in it. These instructions are detailed in their materials, measurements, furnishings and offerings. In fact, the specific instructions fill many chapters in the Book of Exodus.

This man-made sanctuary reflected the heavenly one (Heb. 9:23–24). God warned Moses, "See that you make all things according to the pattern shown you on the mountain" (Heb. 8:5; cf. Exod. 25:40). It was of extreme importance that all was done exactly as shown. This would provide the divine order necessary before the King's glory would be manifested in their presence.

An offering was received from the congregation that supplied all the materials they needed—gold, silver, bronze, blue, purple and scarlet threads, fine linen, skins, fur, acacia wood, oil, spices and precious stones.

The Lord had told Moses:

> See, I have called by name Bezalel…of the tribe of Judah. And I have filled him with the Spirit of God, in wisdom, in understanding, in knowledge, and in all manner of workmanship…And I, indeed I, have appointed with him Aholiab the son of Ahisamach, of the tribe of Dan; and I have put wisdom in the hearts of all who are gifted artisans, that they may make all that I have commanded you.
>
> —Exodus 31:2–3, 6

God's Spirit was on these men to bring divine order. The Spirit of God working through men, joined in harmony with God's Word, would once again bring about divine order.

> ## Once divine order was attained God revealed His glory.

Then all these skilled men began work on the tabernacle. They made the curtains, screens and poles. They forged the ark of the testimony, the table for the shewbread, the gold lamp stand, the altar of incense, the altar of burnt offering, the bronze laver. They made the priestly garments and the anointing oil.

> According to all that the Lord had commanded Moses, so the children of Israel did all the work. Then Moses looked over all the work, and indeed they had done it; as the Lord had commanded, just so they had done it. And Moses blessed them.
>
> Then the LORD spoke to Moses, saying,

> "On the first day of the first month you shall set up the tabernacle of the tent of meeting."
>
> —Exodus 39:42–40:2

God's instructions were so specific that the tabernacle had to be erected on this exact day.

The first day of the first month arrived. Moses and the skilled artisans raised the tabernacle. Then we read:

> So Moses finished the work.
>
> —Exodus 40:33

Everything was ready now. Divine order was in place by the Word of God and a people submitted to the leading of the Holy Spirit. Now notice what happens:

> Then the cloud covered the tabernacle of meeting, and the glory of the Lord filled the tabernacle. And Moses was not able to enter the tabernacle of meeting, because the cloud rested above it, and the glory of the Lord filled the tabernacle.
>
> —Exodus 40:34–35

Once divine order was attained God revealed His glory. Most of us in the church lack an understanding of the glory of the Lord. I have attended many meetings where ministers have declared, either out of ignorance or hype, "The glory of the Lord is here."

Before we proceed further, let's discuss what the glory of the Lord is.

Adapted from *The Fear of the Lord,* 33–38.

TWO

The Glory
of the Lord

DEVELOPING
Inner Strength

God's glory will overcome all other light. He is the perfect and all-consuming light. "They shall go into the holes of the rocks, and into the caves of the earth, from the terror of the LORD and the glory of His majesty, when He arises to shake the earth mightily" (Isa. 2:19).

God's glory is so overpowering that when He came before the children of Israel in the midst of the dark cloud at Sinai, the people cried out in terror and drew back. Moses describes it:

> The LORD spoke to all your assembly, in the mountain from the midst of the fire, the cloud, and the thick darkness, with a loud voice... So it was, when you heard the voice from the midst of the darkness, while the mountain was burning with fire, that you came near to me, all the heads of your tribes and your elders. And you said: "Surely the

LORD our God has shown us His glory and His greatness, and we have heard His voice from the midst of the fire. We have seen this day that God speaks with man; yet he still lives. Now therefore, why should we die? For this great fire will consume us; if we hear the voice of the LORD our God anymore, then we shall die."

—DEUTERONOMY 5:22–25

Though they saw Him shrouded in the thick darkness of a cloud, it could not hide the brilliance of His glory.

The glory of the Lord is not a cloud. Some may ask, "Then why is a cloud mentioned almost every time God's glory is manifested in Scriptures?" The reason: God hides Himself in the cloud. He is too magnificent for mankind to behold. If the cloud did not screen out His countenance, all around Him would be consumed and immediately die.

> And he [Moses] said, "Please, show me Your glory"…But He [God] said, "You cannot see My face; for no man shall see Me, and live."
>
> —Exodus 33:18, 20

Mortal flesh cannot stand in the presence of the holy Lord in His glory. Paul says:

> He who is the blessed and only Potentate, the King of kings and Lord of lords, who alone has immortality, dwelling in unapproachable light, whom no man has seen or can see, to whom be honor and everlasting power. Amen.
>
> —1 Timothy 6:15–16

Hebrews 12:29 tells us that God is a consuming fire. Now when you think of this, do not consider a wood fire. A consuming fire could not be contained in the confines of your fireplace. "God is light and in Him is no darkness at all" (1 John 1:5). The type of fire that burns in your fireplace does not produce perfect light. It contains darkness. It is approachable, and you can look at it.

So let's move on to a more intense light. Consider the laser beam. It is a very focused and intense light, but it is still not perfect light. As bright and powerful as it is, there is darkness in laser light also.

Let's consider the sun. The sun is enormous and unapproachable, bright and powerful, but it still contains darkness within the fire of its light.

Paul says to Timothy that God's glory is "unapproachable light, whom no man has seen or can see."

Paul could very easily write this because he experienced a measure of this light on the road to Damascus. He related it this way to King Agrippa:

> At midday, O king, along the road I saw a light from heaven, brighter than the sun, shining around me.
>
> —Acts 26:13

Paul said this light was brighter than the noon-day sun! Take a moment and try to look directly at the midday sun. It is difficult to look at the sun unless it is veiled with a cloud. God in His glory exceeds this brilliance many fold.

Paul did not see the Lord's face; he saw only the light emanating from Him, for he had to ask, "Who are You, Lord?" He could not see His form or the features of His face. He was blinded by the light that emanated from the Lord's glory, over-whelming even the brightness of the Middle Eastern sun!

> # The glory of the Lord is everything that makes God, God.

Perhaps this explains why both the prophets Joel and Isaiah stated that in the last days when the glory of the Lord is revealed, the sun would be turned into darkness. Isaiah stated, "Behold, the day of the Lord comes…the stars of heaven and their constellations will not give their light; the sun will be darkened in its going forth, and the moon will not cause its light to shine" (Isa. 13:9–10).

All That Makes God, God

So now let's ask the question, What is the glory of the Lord? In answer, we return to Moses' request on the mountain of God. Moses asked:

> Please, show me Your glory.
> —Exodus 33:18

The Hebrew word for *glory* used by Moses in this instance was *kabowd*. It is defined by *Strong's Bible Dictionary* as "the weight of something, but only figuratively in a good sense." Its definition also speaks of splendor, abundance and honor. Moses was asking, "Show me Yourself in *all* your splendor." Look carefully at God's response:

> Then He said, "I will make all My goodness pass before you, and I will proclaim the name of the LORD before you."
> —Exodus 33:19

Moses requested all His glory, and God referred to it as "all My *goodness*…" The Hebrew word for *goodness* is *tuwb*. It means "good in the widest sense." In other words, nothing is withheld.

Then God says, "I will proclaim the name of the LORD before you." Before an earthly king enters the throne room, his name is always announced by proclamation. Then he enters in his splendor. The king's greatness is revealed, and in his court there is no mistake as to who is king. If this monarch were on the street of one of the cities of his nation dressed in ordinary clothes, without any attendants, he might be passed by without those around him realizing his actual identity. So in essence, this is exactly what God did for Moses. He is saying, "I will proclaim My own name and pass by you in all My splendor."

We see then that the glory of the Lord is everything that makes God, God. All His characteristics, authority, power, wisdom—literally the immeasurable weight and magnitude of God—are contained within God's glory. Nothing is hidden or held back!

His Glory Is Revealed in Christ

We are told that the glory of the Lord is revealed in

the face of Jesus Christ (2 Cor. 4:6). Many have claimed to have seen a vision of Jesus and looked upon His face. That is very possible. Paul described it, "For now we see through a glass, darkly; but then face to face" (1 Cor. 13:12, KJV). His glory is veiled by darkened glass, for no man can look upon His fully unveiled glory and live.

Someone else may question, "But the disciples looked at the face of Jesus after He rose from the dead!" That too is correct. The reason it is true is that He did not openly display His glory. There were some who saw the Lord, even in the Old Testament, but He was not revealed in His glory. The Lord appeared to Abraham by the terebinth trees of Mamre (Gen. 18:1–2). Joshua saw the Lord before invading Jericho (Josh. 5:13–14). The Lord said to him, "Take your sandal off your foot, for the place where you stand is holy" (v. 15).

The same is true after the Resurrection. The disciples ate a fish breakfast with Jesus at the Sea of Tiberias (John 21:9–10). Two disciples walked with Jesus on the road to Emmaus, "but their eyes were restrained" (Luke 24:16). These all beheld His face because He did not openly display His glory.

In contrast, John the Apostle saw the Lord in the Spirit and had a totally different encounter than breakfast with Him by the sea, for John saw Him in His glory:

> I was in the Spirit on the Lord's Day, and I heard behind me a loud voice, as of a trumpet…Then I turned to see the voice that spoke with me. And having turned I saw seven golden lampstands, and in the midst of the seven lampstands One like the Son of Man, clothed with a garment down to the feet and girded about the chest with a golden band. His head and hair were white like wool, as white as snow, and His eyes like a flame of fire; His feet were like fine brass, as if refined in a furnace, and His voice as the sound of many waters; He had in His right hand seven stars, out of His mouth went a sharp two-edged sword, and His countenance was like the sun shining in its strength. And when I saw Him, I fell at His feet as dead.
>
> —REVELATION 1:10, 12–17

Notice His countenance was like the sun shining in its strength. How then could John look at Him?

The reason: He was in the Spirit, just as Isaiah was in the Spirit when he saw the throne and the seraphim above it and the One who sat on it (Isa. 6:1–4). Moses could not look upon God's face, for Moses was in his natural physical body.

He Has Withheld His Glory to Test Us

The glory of the Lord is all that makes up God. This far surpasses our ability to comprehend and understand, for even the mighty seraphim continue to cry, "Holy, holy, holy…" in awe and overwhelming wonder.

> He deserves more glory than any living created being can give Him throughout eternity!

The four living creatures before His throne cry, "Holy, holy, holy, Lord God Almighty, who was and is and is to come!" (Rev. 4:8).

> Whenever the living creatures give glory and honor and thanks to Him who sits on the throne, who lives forever and ever, the twenty-four elders fall down before Him who sits on the throne and worship Him who lives forever and ever, and cast their crowns before the throne, saying: "You are worthy, O Lord, to receive glory and honor and power; for You created all things, and by Your will they exist and were created."
>
> —Revelation 4:9–10

He deserves more glory than any living created being can give Him throughout eternity!

We serve the One who created the universe and the earth. He is from everlasting and will be to everlasting! There is no other like Him. In His wisdom, He purposely withholds the revelation of His glory to see if we will serve Him with love and reverence, or if we will turn our attention to that which receives glory on the earth yet pales in comparison to Him.

Adapted from *The Fear of the Lord*, 38–44.

THREE

A New Sanctuary

DEVELOPING
Inner Strength

When Jesus had fulfilled all His Father had ordained for Him to do in His earthly ministry, He was sent to the cross by Caiaphas, the acting high priest, as the sacrificial Lamb. This was the final and most crucial step in the preparation of the temple of the heart of man. Jesus' sacrifice eliminated the sin nature separating man from God's presence since the fall of Adam.

We saw the offering of the sacrificial Lamb foreshadowed in the raising of the tabernacle and the dedication of the temple. When the tabernacle was raised, Aaron, as high priest, made offerings to the Lord. One of the offerings was a lamb without blemish. Once this was done, "Moses and Aaron went into the tabernacle of meeting, and came out and blessed the people. Then the glory of the LORD appeared to all the people" (Lev. 9:23). Shortly after that, Nadab and Abihu were judged and struck dead.

The sacrifice of the Lamb of God is fore-shadowed in the dedication of Solomon's temple.

> *Then the king and all the people offered sacrifices before the L*ORD*. King Solomon offered a sacrifice of twenty-two thousand bulls and one hundred and twenty thousand sheep. So the king and all the people dedicated the house of God.*
>
> —2 CHRONICLES 7:4–5

It was on this same day that the glory of the Lord was revealed in the temple.

The writer of Hebrews compares Christ's sacrifice with those offered in the tabernacle and temple by saying:

> *Not with the blood of goats and calves, but with His own blood He entered the Most Holy Place once for all, having obtained eternal redemption.*
>
> —HEBREWS 9:12

Jesus, the Lamb of God, hung on the cross, shedding every drop of His innocent, royal blood for us. Once this was done, the veil of the temple was torn in two from top to bottom (Luke 23:45). God moved out! God's glory would never again be revealed in a building made with hands. Soon His glory would be revealed in the temple in which He had always longed to dwell.

Under the Old Covenant God's glorious presence dwelled first in the tabernacle, then within the temple of Solomon.

Now God prepares to move into what was always His desired dwelling—a temple not made of stone, but the temple found in the hearts of His sons and daughters.

Make Ready a People Prepared for the Lord

Once again there first had to be divine order. This time the emphasis would not be on outward, but inward order. There in the secret place of the heart would be where the glory of the Lord was next revealed.

This ordering and transforming process began with the ministry of John the Baptist. It would be a mistake to view John as an Old Testament prophet, for the Bible describes his ministry as "the beginning of the gospel of Jesus Christ" (Mark 1:1). His preaching is found at the beginning of all four Gospels. Jesus reemphasized this by declaring, "The law and the prophets were until John" (Luke 16:16). Notice that He did not say,

"The law and the prophets were until *Me*."

John's birth was announced to his father by an angel. His ministry's thrust was summed up by these words: "And he will turn many of the children of Israel to the Lord their God…to make ready a people prepared for the Lord" (Luke 1:16-17).

Notice he was "to make ready a people prepared for the Lord." Just as God had anointed the artisans and craftsmen in the days of Moses to build the tabernacle, so He anointed John to prepare the temple not made with hands. By the Spirit of God, he began the process of preparation for the new temple.

Isaiah prophesied of John:

> The voice of one crying in the wilderness: "Prepare the way of the LORD…every valley shall be exalted and every mountain and hill brought low; the crooked places shall be made straight and the rough places smooth; the glory of the LORD shall be revealed."
>
> —ISAIAH 40:3–5

These mountains and hills were not fortresses of natural elements, but rather the ways of man that opposed the ways of God. The towering and lofty pride of men had to be made low. The irreverence and foolishness of man would be confronted and leveled in preparation for the revelation of the glory of the Lord.

The Hebrew word for *crooked* in the above verse is *aqob*. *Strong's* defines it as "fraudulent, deceitful, polluted or crooked." It is easy to see that "crooked" does not refer to a lack of physical straightness. A more accurate translation of the word *aqob* would be "deceitful."

John was not sent to those who did not know the name of the Lord. He was sent to those in covenant with Jehovah. Israel had become religious, yet believed everything was fine. In truth God saw the Israelites as lost sheep. The thousands who faithfully attended the synagogue remained unaware of their true heart condition. They were deceived and thought their worship and service to be acceptable to God.

John exposed this deceit and tore aside the shroud of such deception. He shook the unstable foundation on which they had justified themselves as Abraham's seed. He brought to light the error in the doctrines of their elders and exposed their formula prayers void of passion and power. He showed the futility of paying tithes while neglecting and even robbing the poor. He pointed out the emptiness of their lifeless religious habits and clearly revealed that their hardened hearts were far from God.

> The lofty mountains of pride and haughty hills of religion were made flat, preparing the people to receive the ministry of Jesus.

John came preaching a baptism of repentance (Mark 1:4). The Greek word for *baptism* is *baptisma* and is defined as "immersion." According to Webster's, *immersion* means "to plunge." So John's message was not of partial repentance but of a radical, complete change of heart.

John's bold confrontations destroyed the false security the Israelites had found in their firmly rooted deceptions. His message was a call for men to turn their hearts back to God. His divine assignment leveled the ground of the hearts that received him. The lofty mountains of pride and haughty hills of religion were made flat, preparing the people to receive the ministry of Jesus.

The Master Builder

Once John's work was complete, Jesus came to prepare the temple on the level ground of humility until the building process was complete. Jesus laid the foundation and built: "For no other foundation can anyone lay than that which is laid, which is Jesus Christ" (1 Cor. 3:11).

Once again God's Word brought divine order. But this time His Word was revealed as God's Word made flesh! Jesus is the Master Builder (Heb. 3:1–4), not only by His teachings, but also in the life He lived. In every way He showed forth to mankind the acceptable way of the Lord.

Those who received John's ministry were ready to receive the work of their Master Builder. Conversely, those who rejected John were unprepared to receive the words of Jesus, for the ground of their hearts was uneven and unstable. No foundation had been laid. They were unprepared building sites incapable of supporting a sanctuary.

Jesus addressed the religious proud that resisted Him: "For John came to you in the way of righteousness, and you did not believe him; but tax collectors and harlots believed him; and when you saw it, you did not afterward relent and believe him" (Matt. 21:32). It was the sinners of the day who received the message of John and in turn opened their hearts to Jesus. "Then all the tax collectors and the sinners drew near to Him [Jesus] to hear Him" (Luke 15:1). They were not comforted in their religion and knew they needed a Savior.

It was then that God's eternal plan for redemption for fallen and sinful man was unveiled. As we read in the opening vignette of this chapter, Jesus' work of salvation through His sacrifice on the cross of Calvary was the final step in the preparation of the temple of the heart of man. The earthly temple was no longer the dwelling place of God. Never again would a building contain God's glory. God's temple would now become the heart of man, and His glory would be revealed through man.

One in Heart and Purpose

Now read what happened shortly after the resurrection of Jesus:

> When the Day of Pentecost had fully come, they were all with one accord in one place. And suddenly there came a sound from heaven, as of a rushing mighty wind, and it filled the whole house where they were sitting. Then there appeared to them divided tongues, as of fire, and one sat upon each of them.
>
> —ACTS 2:1–3

Once again the glory of the Lord is manifested. Notice, "they were all with one accord." *Divine order.* How do you get a hundred and twenty into one accord? The answer is simple. They were all dead to themselves. They had no agendas. All that mattered was that they had obeyed the words of Jesus.

We know Jesus ministered to tens of thousands in His three-and-a-half-year ministry. Multitudes followed Him. After His crucifixion and resurrection He appeared to more than five hundred followers (1 Cor. 15:6). Yet on the Day of Pentecost, we find only a hundred and twenty in the house when the Spirit of God fell (Acts 1:15).

It is interesting to note that the numbers kept decreasing, not increasing. Where were the thousands after the Crucifixion? Why did He appear to only five hundred? On the Day of Pentecost, where were the five hundred? Why was God's glory revealed to only one hundred twenty followers?

> # Jesus' work of salvation through His sacrifice on the cross of Calvary was the final step in the preparation of the temple of the heart of man.

After His resurrection Jesus told the people not to depart from Jerusalem, but to wait for the promise of the Father (Acts 1:4). I believe that all five hundred initially waited for the promise. But as the days passed, the size of the group dwindled. Impatient, some may have decided, "We have to go on with our lives; He is gone." Others may have left to worship God in their synagogue in the traditional manner.

Still others may have quoted the words of Jesus, "We must go into all the world and preach the gospel. We'd better leave now and do it!"

I believe the Lord waited until those who remained had the resolve to say within themselves, *If we rot, we are not moving, for the Master said wait.* Only those who were completely submitted to the Master could make such a commitment. No person, activity or thing mattered as much as obedience to His words. These were the ones who trembled at His Word (Isa. 66:2). They feared God!

Those who remained had listened intently when Jesus spoke to the multitude saying:

> And whoever does not bear his cross and come after Me cannot be My disciple. For which of you, intending to build a tower, does not sit down first and count the cost, whether he has enough to finish it—lest, after he has laid the foundation, and is not able to finish, all who see it begin to mock him, saying, "This man began to build and was not able to finish"…So likewise, whoever of you does not forsake all that he has cannot be My disciple.
>
> —Luke 14:27–30, 33

Jesus makes it clear that to follow Him, we must first count the cost. There is a price to following Jesus, and He makes the amount certain. The price is nothing short of our lives!

You may question, "I thought salvation was a free gift, one you cannot earn?" Yes, salvation is a gift that cannot be bought or earned. However, you cannot retain it if you do not give your entire life in exchange for it! Even a gift must be protected from being lost or stolen.

Jesus exhorts, "But he who endures to the end will be saved" (Matt. 10:22). The strength to endure is found in freely giving up your life.

A true believer, a disciple, lays down his life completely for the Master. Disciples are steadfast to the end. Converts and onlookers may desire the benefits and blessings, but they lack the endurance to last to the end. Eventually they will fade away. Jesus gave the Great Commission to "go therefore and make disciples of all the nations" (Matt. 28:19). He commissioned us to make disciples, not converts.

The remnant who remained on the Day of Pentecost had laid aside their dreams, ambitions, goals and agendas. This created an atmosphere where they could be of one purpose and one heart.

This is the unity God desires to bring us into today. There have been various moves for unity in our cities among some leaders and churches. We come together and seek oneness.

> # We can have unity of purpose without obedience to the heart of our Master. Then our productivity is in vain.

But we must remember that only God can truly make us one. Unless we have laid all else aside, eventually agendas that were hidden will surface. When there are hidden motives, relationships are developed on a superficial level. The outcome is shallow and nonproductive. We can have unity of purpose without obedience to the heart of our Master. Then our productivity is in vain. For, "unless the Lord builds the house, they labor in vain who build it" (Ps. 127:1). God is still looking for those who tremble at His Word! That is where true unity is found.

The Glory of the Lord Revealed

Those together on the Day of Pentecost had true unity. They were one in the purpose of their Master. Their hearts were in order. The preparation of John's ministry had coupled with the ministry of Jesus, and divine order resulted. Divine order was achieved in the hearts of men. In line with the pattern of God, after divine order came God's revealed glory. Read again what happened that day:

> And suddenly there came a sound from heaven, as of a rushing mighty wind, and it filled the whole house where they were sitting. Then there appeared to them divided tongues, as of fire, and one sat upon each of them.
>
> —Acts 2:2–3

A measure of God's glory manifested on these one hundred twenty men and women. Notice that tongues as of fire rested upon each one. Forget images you have seen in your Sunday school books—the little flames of fire floating above the heads of these disciples. Everyone present was baptized or immersed in the fire of His glorious presence (Matt. 3:11).

Of course, this was not God's full, unveiled glory, for no man has seen nor can he withstand God's full, unveiled glory (1 Tim. 6:16). Yet this manifestation was strong enough to attract the attention of multitudes of devout, God-fearing Jews residing in Jerusalem from every country under heaven (Acts 2:6–7).

In answer at this point, Peter stood and preached the gospel to them. That day three thousand were saved and added to the church. It was not a scheduled service, nor had there been any advertisement. As a result:

> Then fear came upon every soul, and many wonders and signs were done through the apostles.
>
> —ACTS 2:43

God had revealed a portion of His glory, and the people were in awe of His presence and power. He continued to work in a mighty way. Daily there were testimonies of tremendous miracles and deliverances.

There was no denying God's mighty hand at work. Men and women came into the kingdom in droves. Those who had previously given their lives to Jesus were refreshed by the presence of His Spirit.

But as we have already seen, if God reveals His glory and the people return to a lack of fear, there is certain judgment. In fact, the greater the glory, the greater and swifter the judgment.

Adapted from *The Fear of the Lord*, 57–65.

FOUR

Judgment for Irreverence

DEVELOPING
Inner Strength

God had instructed Moses, "Now take Aaron your brother, and his sons with him, from among the children of Israel, that he may minister to Me as priest, Aaron and Aaron's sons: Nadab, Abihu, Eleazar, and Ithamar" (Exod. 28:1).

These men were set apart and trained to minister to the Lord and stand in the gap for the people. Their duties and parameters for worship were outlined in very specific instructions passed on from God to Moses. Their training was a part of divine order. Following this instruction and training came the actual consecration of these men. With everything in place, their ministry began.

Read carefully what two of these priests did after the glory of the Lord had been revealed in the tabernacle: "Nadab and Abihu, the sons of Aaron, each took his censer and put fire in it, put incense on it, and offered profane fire before the

LORD, which He had not commanded them" (Lev. 10:1).

Notice Nadab and Abihu offered profane fire before the presence of the Lord. One definition for *profane* in *Webster's Dictionary* is "showing disrespect or contempt for sacred things; irreverent."

It means to treat what God calls holy or sacred as if it were common. These two men grabbed the censers that were set apart for the worship of the Lord and filled them with the fire and incense of their choosing, not the offering prescribed by God. They were careless with what God had called holy and exhibited a lack of reverence. They came with irreverence into the presence of the Lord, bearing an unacceptable offering. They treated what was holy as common. Look what happened as a result: "So fire went out from the Lord and devoured them, and they died before the Lord" (Lev. 10:2).

These two men were instantly judged for their irreverence. They were met with immediate death. Their irreverence took place after the revelation of God's glory. Though they were priests, they were not exempt from rendering God honor. They sinned by approaching a holy God as though He were common! They had become too familiar with His presence!

Once the tabernacle was erected, divine order was achieved. As soon as everything was in place, "Then the cloud covered the tabernacle of meeting, and the glory of the Lord filled the tabernacle. And Moses was not able to enter the tabernacle of meeting, because the cloud rested above it, and the glory of the Lord filled the tabernacle"(Exod. 40:34–35). We can understand why even God's friend, Moses, could not enter in. The tabernacle was permeated with the glory of the Lord!

God's glory manifesting and abiding among Israel brought tremendous blessing. In His glorious presence were provision, guidance, healing and protection. No enemy could stand before Israel. The revelation of His Word was abundant. There was also the benefit of having the cloud of His glory to shade the children of Israel from the heat of the desert by day, as well as to provide warmth and light for them at night. There was no lack of anything they needed.

Judgment

However, even though God's glory had manifested

to the children of Israel, judgment soon followed. As we read in the opening vignette of this chapter, Nadab and Abihu offered an irreverent offering before God—and encountered the swift hand of God's judgment. Immediately after their death, Moses spoke to Aaron regarding such irreverence:

> And Moses said to Aaron, "This is what the LORD spoke, saying: 'By those who come near Me I must be regarded as holy; and before all the people I must be glorified.'" So Aaron held his peace.
>
> —LEVITICUS 10:3

God had already made it clear that irreverence could not survive in the presence of a holy God. God is not mocked. Today is no different; He is the same holy God. We cannot expect to be admitted into His presence with an attitude of disrespect.

Nadab and Abihu were Moses' nephews. But Moses knew better than to question God's judgment, for he knew God to be just. In fact, Moses warned Aaron and his two surviving sons not to even mourn Nadab and Abihu lest they die as well. Such mourning would have further dishonored the Lord, so the bodies of Nadab and Abihu were carried outside the camp and buried.

Once again, we see the pattern—divine order, God's revealed glory, then judgment for irreverence.

A New Sanctuary

Almost five hundred years later, King David's son Solomon began a temple for the presence of the Lord. This was a massive undertaking. The store of materials, most of which were gathered under the reign of David, was enormous.

Before his death, David instructed Solomon:

> I have worked hard to provide materials for building the Temple of the LORD—nearly four thousand tons of gold, nearly forty thousand tons of silver, and so much iron and bronze that it cannot be weighed. I have also gathered lumber and stone for the walls, though you may need to add more.
>
> You have many skilled stonemasons and carpenters and craftsmen of every kind available to you. They are expert goldsmiths and silversmiths and workers of bronze and iron. Now begin the work, and may the LORD be with you!
>
> —1 CHRONICLES 22:14–16, NLT

Solomon added to the materials already provided and began the temple in the fourth year of his reign. The design of the temple was magnificent, its ornamentation and detail extraordinary. Even with a task force of tens of thousands of men, the gathering of materials and construction still took seven full years. We then read:

> So all the work that Solomon had done for the house of the LORD was finished.
>
> —2 CHRONICLES 5:1

Solomon then gathered Israel to Jerusalem where the temple stood. "Then the priests brought in the ark of the covenant of the LORD to its place" (2 Chron. 5:7). All the priests sanctified themselves. There would be no irreverence in the presence of God. They remembered the fate of their distant relatives Nadab and Abihu.

Then the Levites who were the singers and musicians stood at the east end of the altar, clothed in white linen. With them were one hundred twenty priests, sounding with trumpets.

Once again, great care, time and an enormous amount of work and preparation brought divine order. And what came after divine order? Let's read:

Indeed it came to pass, when the trumpeters and singers were as one, to make one sound to be heard in praising and thanking the LORD, and when they lifted up their voice with the trumpets and cymbals and instruments of music, and praised the LORD, saying: "For He is good, for His mercy endures forever," that the house, the house of the LORD, was filled with a cloud, so that the priests could not continue ministering because of the cloud; for the glory of the LORD filled the house of God.

—2 CHRONICLES 5:13–14

When divine order was achieved, the glory of the Lord was revealed. Again it was so overwhelming that the priests were unable to minister for the glory of the Lord filled the temple.

Judgment

Following this revelation of God's glory, we again see irreverence toward His presence and Word. Though the Israelites knew His will, their hearts grew careless toward what God calls sacred and holy.

Moreover all the leaders of the priests and the people transgressed more and more, according to all the abominations of the nations, and defiled the house of the LORD which He had consecrated in Jerusalem. And the LORD God of their fathers sent warnings to them by His messengers, rising up early and sending them, because He had compassion on His people and on His dwelling place. But they mocked the messengers of God, despised His words, and scoffed at His prophets.

—2 CHRONICLES 36:14–16

They ridiculed His messengers and disregarded their words of warning. The people mocked His prophets. I have seen the same evidence of a great lack of fear today.

> Great care, time and an enormous amount of work and preparation brought divine order.

Recently I ministered at a large church, preaching a strong message on obedience and the lordship of Jesus. The wife of one of our staff members had left the service with her baby and gone to the lobby where the service was airing on closed-circuit television. She overheard two women of the church discussing the sermon: "Who does he think he is? Turn him off!" they scoffed.

Where is the fear of the Lord?

Israel and Judah suffered repeated judgment due to their lack of fear and respect for God's sacred presence and His Word. Their judgment climaxed when Abraham's descendants were carried off into Babylonian captivity. Read this account:

> But they mocked the messengers of God, despised His words, and scoffed at His prophets, until the wrath of the LORD arose against His people, till there was no remedy.
>
> Therefore He brought against them the king of the Chaldeans, who killed their young men with the sword in the house of their sanctuary, and had no compassion on young man or virgin, on the aged or the weak; He [God] gave them all into his hand. And all the articles from the house of God, great and small, the treasures of the house of the LORD, and the treasures of the king

and of his leaders, all these he took to Babylon. Then they burned the house of God, broke down the wall of Jerusalem, burned all its palaces with fire, and destroyed all its precious possessions.

—2 Chronicles 36:16–19

I want you to think carefully about what I am about to say. We have retraced three accounts—the garden, the tabernacle and the temple. In every case the judgment was severe. Each resulted in death and destruction.

What is most sobering is the fact that we are not talking about people who had never experienced God's glory or His presence. These judgments were against those who not only had heard His Word, but had also walked in His presence and experienced His glory!

Adapted from *The Fear of the Lord*, 47–53.

FIVE

An Irreverent Offering

DEVELOPING
Inner Strength

In August 1995, I ministered for a week of meetings in Kuala Lumpur, Malaysia. The atmosphere had been very difficult, and on the last day I sensed that we had finally experienced a breakthrough. The presence of the Lord filled the building, and several people laughed as His joy flowed. This continued for ten to fifteen minutes; then there was a pause followed by another wave of God's presence. More were touched. Again, there was a lull; then another wave of God's presence washed in with a joy that permeated the sanctuary until nearly everyone was refreshed and laughing. Then there was yet another break.

It was then that I heard the Lord say, "I am coming in one last wave, but it will be different than the others." I kept silent and waited. Within minutes a very different manifestation of God's presence permeated the building. It was awesome and almost frightening. Yet I was drawn to it. The atmosphere became charged. The same people who had been laughing only moments earlier began to weep, wail and cry. Some even screamed as though they were on fire. Yet these were not the tormented screams of demonic activity.

As I paced the platform, this thought went through my mind: *John, don't make one wrong move or say one wrong word. If you do, you're a dead man.* I'm not certain that would have happened, but this thought relays the intensity I felt. I knew irreverence could not exist in this awesome presence. I witnessed two different responses that day—either the people were afraid and drew away from His presence, or they feared God and drew close to His awesome presence. This was definitely not one of those times when God was whispering, "Come, jump in My lap!"

We left the meeting shrouded in awe. Many felt completely transformed by the awesome presence of God. One man who was mightily touched by His presence said to me afterward, "I feel so clean inside." I agreed, for I felt purged as well. Later I found this scripture: "The fear of the LORD is clean, enduring forever" (Ps. 19:9).

Time had passed since the Day of Pentecost. The church had benefited from the presence of God and His power. Multitudes were saved; others were healed and delivered. No one lacked, for everyone shared what they had. Those with possessions sold them and brought the proceeds to the apostles for distribution to those in need.

Offering From a Foreigner

And Joses, who was also named Barnabas by the apostles (which is translated Son of Encouragement), a Levite of the country of Cyprus, having land, sold it, and brought the money and laid it at the apostles' feet.
—Acts 4:36–37

Cyprus was an island abundantly blessed with natural resources, famous for its flowers and fruits. Wine and oil were produced in abundance. There was a store of a variety of precious stones. But its chief source of wealth lay in its mines and forests. There were extensive silver, copper and iron mines. It was a country overflowing in natural wealth. If you owned land on Cyprus, you were probably wealthy.

Picture this: A wealthy Levite from another land, named Barnabas, brought the total amount he received for the sale of his land, which was probably a very large sum, and placed it at the apostles' disposal. Now read carefully the next verse:

> But a certain man named Ananias, with Sapphira his wife, sold a possession.
>
> —ACTS 5:1

Notice the first word of this sentence, "But." In the Bible, no new thought is introduced with the word *but*. Remember, the translators were the people who separated each book of the Bible by chapter and verse. Originally the Book of Acts was just one big letter written by a doctor named Luke.

By usage of the word *but*, it is obvious that what had just happened in the fourth chapter of Acts is tied to the record of Ananias and Sapphira in the fifth chapter. In fact, I will be bold enough to say that you cannot fully understand what is about to take place without taking into account what previously happened. It would explain the reason for the word *but* at the beginning of the sentence.

Let us think this through together. A newcomer

who is very wealthy joins the church and brings a very large offering from a piece of land he has sold. This man's offering causes Ananias and Sapphira to react by selling something they own. Examine the next few verses carefully:

> And he kept back part of the proceeds, his wife also being aware of it, and brought a certain part and laid it at the apostles' feet. But Peter said, "Ananias, why has Satan filled your heart to lie to the Holy Spirit and keep back part of the price of the land for yourself? While it remained, was it not your own? And after it was sold, was it not in your own control? Why have you conceived this thing in your heart? You have not lied to men but to God."
>
> —Acts 5:2–4

Up to this point, Ananias and his wife most likely had the reputation in the church of being the biggest givers. They had probably received much attention from the people for their generosity. In seeing their response, I am certain that they thoroughly enjoyed this position of respect and the recognition they received for their ministry of giving.

Now they had been outdone. The attention had shifted to this new man, the Levite from Cyprus. Everyone was extolling the virtues of this generous man. The people conversed among themselves extensively about how his great gift would help so many in need. It was the talk of the church. The light of attention had been diverted from Ananias and Sapphira, creating a void they could not deal with.

> **If you desire the praise of man, you will fear man. If you fear man, you will serve him—for you will serve what you fear.**

They responded by immediately selling a plot of land. It was also valuable, and they received a large sum of money. It was probably their prize possession. Together they must have concluded, "This is far too much money to part with. We cannot give it all. But we want to *appear* to be giving it all. So let's give only part of it and say that it is everything we received."

Together they agreed to withhold some of the profit for themselves. But they still wanted to appear as if they had given the entire amount. Deception was their sin. It was not wrong to keep some of the proceeds from the sale. The money was theirs to do with as they wished. But it was wrong to say they had given all they'd received, when in fact that was a lie. They wanted the praises of man more than truth and integrity. Their reputations were important to them. They must have comforted themselves by saying, "What could it hurt? We're giving and meeting the needs of those less fortunate. That is the bottom line."

If you desire the praise of man, you will fear man. If you fear man, you will serve him—for you will serve what you fear. They feared man more than God. This caused them to reason away their actions and stand in the presence of God void of holy fear. If they were afraid of God, they never would have lied in His presence.

> Then Ananias, hearing these words, fell down and breathed his last. So great fear

came upon all those who heard these things. And the young men arose and wrapped him up, carried him out, and buried him.

—Acts 5:5–6

This man brought an offering for the needy and wound up falling over dead! Immediate judgment occurred. Great fear came upon all those who witnessed or heard about it. Continue reading:

Now it was about three hours later when his wife came in, not knowing what had happened. And Peter answered her, "Tell me whether you sold the land for so much?" She said, "Yes, for so much." Then Peter said to her, "How is it that you have agreed together to test the Spirit of the Lord? Look, the feet of those who have buried your husband are at the door, and they will carry you out." Then immediately she fell down at his feet and breathed her last. And the young men came in and found her dead, and carrying her out, buried her by her husband. So great fear came upon all the church and upon all who heard these things.

—Acts 5:7–11

It is quite possible that Ananias and his wife were some of the first to receive salvation through grace. They may have been the biggest givers in the church. They may have sacrificed their social standing and financial security in service to God. But sacrifices are useless when unaccompanied by hearts that love and fear God.

Notice the last verse of scripture: "So great fear came upon all the church." Recall God's warning to Aaron when his two sons had died in the presence of God while presenting their offerings without reverence.

> By those who come near Me I must be regarded as holy; and before all the people I must be glorified.
>
> —Leviticus 10:3

Over the centuries God had not changed. His Word and level of holiness had not varied. His Word had not faltered since its release some two thousand years before. God was, is and will always be the great King, and He must be reverenced as such. We cannot treat what He calls holy lightly.

The Bible doesn't say great fear came upon the *city,* but rather great fear came upon the *church.*

The church was enjoying the presence of the Lord and all His benefits. When the people were filled with the Holy Spirit they acted like drunk men. I'm sure some laughed with joy and the wonder of it all as they all spoke in tongues. Why else would they have been mistaken for being drunk at nine o'clock in the morning (Acts 2:15)?

> God was, is and will always be the great King, and He must be reverenced as such.

Perhaps with the passage of time the people became too familiar with the presence of God. It became common to some of them. Maybe they remembered how approachable Jesus had been and decided now that their relationship with the Holy Spirit would become similar. Although Jesus is the Son and the express image of God made flesh, we cannot forget He came as the Son of man, and mediator, because man *could not* approach the holiness of God.

Though they are one, there is a differential

between God the Father, God the Son and God the Holy Spirit. Even Jesus said that men could speak against Him and it would be forgiven them, but not if they spoke against the Holy Spirit. Jesus was letting them know ahead of time that a holy, divine order was about to be restored. Before the coming of the Son, the people had been afraid or scared of God, but they did not fear Him. Now man was restored to God, and divine order had to be reestablished.

The church wakes up to the holiness of God when Ananias and Sapphira fall dead at Peter's feet. *Maybe we should rethink some things,* some may have wondered. Others may have thought, *That easily could have been me.* Others had their concept of God jolted! *I guess I don't know Him as well as I thought I did. I would not have thought Him to bring such swift and severe judgment.* But everyone exclaimed in wonder and amazement, "He is holy and all knowing!" Great fear came upon all the church as they searched their hearts, amazed by this God of awe and wonder, so loving and yet so holy. No one remained unaffected by this startling event.

Conduct Yourselves in the Fear of God

Peter, who walked with Jesus and also witnessed this judgment, later wrote by inspiration this heartfelt admonishment:

> He who called you is holy, you also be holy in all your conduct, because it is written, "Be holy, for I am holy." And if you call on the Father, who without partiality judges according to each one's work, conduct yourselves throughout the time of your stay here in fear.
>
> —1 Peter 1:15–17

Notice he does not say "conduct yourselves in love." Yes, we are to walk in love, for without it we have nothing! Apart from His love, we cannot even know the Father's heart. Earlier in this very epistle, Peter comments on the love that is to burn in our hearts for the Lord, "whom having not seen you love" (1 Pet. 1:8). We are called to have a personal love relationship with our Father, but Peter is quick to add the balance of the fear of God. Our love for God is limited by a lack of holy fear. Our hearts are to bear the light and warmth of both flames.

You may wonder how this love could be limited. You can only love someone to the extent that you know them. If your image of God falls short of who He is, then you have but a surface knowledge of the One you love. True love is founded in the truth of who God really is. Do you think He reveals His heart to those who take Him lightly? *Would you?* In fact, God has chosen to hide Himself (Isa. 45:15). The psalmist refers to His place of hiding as "the secret place" (Ps. 91:1).

> # We are to walk in love, for without it we have nothing!

It is here in secret that we discover His holiness and His greatness. But only those who fear Him will find this secret refuge. For we are told:

> The secret of the LORD is with those who fear Him, and He will show them His covenant.
>
> —PSALM 25:14

Now you can more fully understand Peter's words. Paul, who did not walk with Jesus on earth but met Him on the road to Damascus, fortified this exhortation by adding the word *trembling*. He says to the believers, "Work out your own salvation with fear and trembling" (Phil. 2:12). This phrase is used three times in the New Testament to describe the proper relationship between a believer and Christ.

Paul came to know Jesus by revelation of the Spirit. This is the same way we are to come to know Him. "Even though we have known Christ according to the flesh, yet now we know Him thus no longer" (2 Cor. 5:16). If we seek to access the knowledge of God and walk with Him as we walk with natural, corruptible men, we will eventually take His presence for granted, as some did in the early church.

I'm sure Ananias and Sapphira were a part of those who were astonished and excited in the early church of Acts. All had been amazed by the abundant signs and wonders. Yet even signs and wonders will become commonplace when there is a lack of the fear of God in hearts. The fear of God would have restrained the foolishness of this unfortunate couple. (See Psalm 34:11–13.) The fear would have revealed the holiness of God.

We must remember both of these unchangeable attributes: "God is love," and "God is a consuming fire" (1 John 4:8; Heb. 12:29). Paul refers to the fire experienced by believers when they stand before a holy God at the judgment seat. There we will give account of our works done in the body of Christ, both good and bad (2 Cor. 5:10). Paul then warns, "Knowing, therefore, the terror of the Lord, we persuade men…" (2 Cor. 5:11).

Because of God's love, we can have confidence when we approach Him. The Bible adds that we must serve and approach Him acceptably. How? With reverence and godly fear (Heb. 12:28).

Those who have been born again know God as Abba Father. But that does not negate His position as Judge of all flesh (Gal. 4:6–7; Heb. 12:23). God makes it clear: "The LORD will judge His people" (Heb. 10:30).

Consider an earthly king with sons and daughters. In the palace, he is husband and Dad. But in the throne room, he is king and must be reverenced as such even by his wife and children. Yes, there are those times when I have sensed the

Father call to me from His private chamber, arms outstretched, inviting me to "come, jump on My lap, and let's embrace and talk." I love those times. They are so special. But there are times when I am praying or participating in a service when I have feared and trembled at His holy presence. Our opening vignette for this chapter describes one such service.

The Fear of the Lord Endures

The fear of the Lord *does* endure forever! If Lucifer had possessed it, he would never have fallen from heaven like lightning (Isa. 14:12–15; Luke 10:18). Lucifer was the anointed cherub on the holy mountain of God and walked in the presence of the Lord (Ezek. 28:14–17). Yet Lucifer was the first one to exhibit a lack of the fear of God.

Hear me, people of God: You can have the holy anointing oil on you, just as Nadab and Abihu did. You can operate in signs and wonders, cast out demons and heal the sick in His mighty name, yet lack the fear of the Lord! Without it your end will be no different than that of Nadab and Abihu, or of Ananias and Sapphira. For it is the fear of the

Lord that causes you to stand before the presence of the Lord forever!

Adam and Eve walked in the presence of the Lord. They loved and benefited from His goodness. They had never been offended by any authority. They lived in a perfect environment. Yet they disobeyed and fell, suffering great judgment. They would never have fallen if they had possessed the fear of the Lord.

The fear of the Lord *does* endure forever! If Ananias and Sapphira had feared God, they would not have behaved so foolishly, for "by the fear of the LORD one departs from evil" (Prov. 16:6).

> ## It is the fear of the Lord that causes you to stand before the presence of the Lord forever!

Some may question, "Doesn't my love for God keep me from sin?" Yes, but how extensive can this love be when you lack the fear of Him?

When I visited Jim Bakker while he was still in prison, he shared with me how the heat of prison had caused him to experience a complete change of heart. While in prison, he experienced Jesus as the Master for the first time. He shared how he had lost his family, ministry and everything he owned, and then found Jesus.

I remember his words distinctly: "John, this prison is not God's judgment on my life but His mercy. I believe if I had continued on the path I was on, I would have ended up in hell!"

Then Jim Bakker shared this warning for all of us: "John, I always loved Jesus, yet He was not my Lord, and there are millions of Americans just like me!" Jim loved the image of Jesus that had been revealed to him. His love had been immature for it lacked the fear of the Lord. Today Jim Bakker is a man who fears God. Because my visit took place before his release from prison, I asked him what he would do when he got out. He quickly replied, "If I go back to the way I was, I will be judged!" In the years since his release he has continued to show the evidence of his understanding of the importance of the fear of the Lord in his life.

No One Dared Join Them

What happened to Ananias and Sapphira shook the church. It brought motives of the heart to the surface for inspection. Those who saw themselves in the irreverence of Ananias and Sapphira rent their hearts in repentance. Others counted the cost more seriously before joining themselves with the assembly of believers in Jerusalem. Some may have walked away in fear of God's judgment.

> When irreverence is judged, everyone takes stock of their lives, and wrong motives are purged by the light of judgment.

Fear came upon the church, but it also awed all who heard what had happened to this couple. I'm sure it was news for some time in the city. People questioned each other, "Did you hear what happened to those followers of Jesus? A couple brought

an offering for the needy and fell over dead!" The
Bible records:

> None of the rest dared join them, but the
> people esteemed them highly. And believers
> were increasingly added to the Lord, multi-
> tudes of both men and women
>
> —ACTS 5:13–14

It would seem to be a contradiction: None dared
to join, yet the next verse states that believers were
increasingly added. How can believers be added
when no one will join? What is actually being said
here? I believe that no one dared to join themselves
to Jesus until they had counted the cost. There was
no more "joining" for self-seeking reasons. They
came to the Lord because of who He was, not
because of what He could do.

It is easy to develop quickly an attitude of irreverence when we come to the Lord for what He can
do for us or give to us. It is a relationship based on
blessings and events. When things don't go our
way—and inevitably this will happen—we're disappointed, and like spoiled children, our respect is
gone. When irreverence is judged, everyone takes
stock of their lives, and wrong motives are purged

by the light of judgment. This is an atmosphere for true hearts of repentance filled with the fear of God.

Why Them?

Why did Ananias and Sapphira die? I know people who have lied to preachers, and they haven't been judged so severely. In fact, there have been many more irreverent acts than that of Ananias and Sapphira in church history and even in the church today. No one drops dead in services any more. The whole event seems so impossible today.

The answer is found hidden in the verses immediately following this account:

> They brought the sick out into the streets and laid them on beds and couches, that at least the shadow of Peter passing by might fall on some of them.
>
> —Acts 5:15

Notice they laid the sick in the *streets!* Not street, but streets—just waiting for the shadow of Peter to pass by so the sick could be healed. Now I realize what I am about to say is subject to argument, but I believe that interpretation was not limited to Peter's physical shadow alone. A shadow holds no power to heal the sick. I believe it was the cloud of God. The Lord's presence was so strong on Peter that a cloud shadowed and veiled Peter's own shadow. In the same way, when Moses came down from the mountain of God, the glory of God was shining from his face so that his own image was veiled by it. Could it be that God Himself had veiled Peter in a cloud of shadow to hide His glory? In Acts 5:15, all Peter had to do was come within a shadow's range of the sick, and multitudes on the streets were healed.

We know that a very tangible presence of God's glory rested on Peter when first Ananias and then Sapphira lied to Peter and fell over dead. In essence, Ananias and Sapphira fell over dead because they were irreverent in the presence of the Lord whose glory had been revealed already. Just as with Adam, Nadab, Abihu and the children of Israel, once again we see the pattern of order, glory and judgment.

Adapted from *The Fear of the Lord*, 69–80.

Conclusion

In this book, we've been able to glimpse how glorious the Acts church was during the former rain of God's Spirit. But how does today's church compare with the Book of Acts? There is no way to compare today's church to the glorious church of Acts. We may have more *resources,* but it seems that we have less of the *source.* I am not against books, tapes, television, computers and satellite technology. These are all resources, but if they are not breathed upon by the Source, they will fall short. *God is the Source for all our resources.*

God is challenging us to increase our vision. Proverbs 29:18 tells us, "Where there is no revelation [prophetic vision], the people cast off restraint." With this revelation of our need, He makes a way for His prophetic vision. Read God's Word and see His vision:

"The glory of this latter temple shall be

greater than the former," says the LORD of hosts.

—HAGGAI 2:9

Wow! Can you envision that? God says His revealed glory will *exceed* that displayed in the Book of Acts! Do you see how short of God's vision we still are?

In fact, the Lord stunned me by speaking to me in prayer a few years ago: "John, the magnitude of My revealed glory in the coming days shall be seven times greater than what the people experienced in the Book of Acts!"

The latter rain will be poured out all over the earth in a much greater measure!

I immediately cried out, "Lord, I don't know that I can believe or comprehend that! I need to see what You have just spoken in Your Word to confirm that this is You speaking to me."

I have done this often, and the Lord has never chastened me for it. Scripture says, "By the mouth of two or three witnesses every word shall be established" (2 Cor. 13:1). The Spirit of God does not contradict His written, established Word.

The Lord immediately responded, rapidly dropping scriptures into my heart—not just two or three but several.

First He asked, "John, did I not say in My Word that when the thief is caught, he must restore sevenfold (Prov. 6:31)? The thief has stolen from the church, but My Word says that heaven must receive Jesus until the times of restoration of *all* things! That restoration will be sevenfold!"

He continued, "John, did not I say in My Word that I would cause the enemies that rose against my people to be defeated? 'They shall come out against you one way and flee before you seven ways'" (Deut. 28:7).

Then, using a verse from Ecclesiastes, He asked, "John, did not I say in My Word that 'The end of a thing is better than its beginning' (Eccles. 7:8)? The end of the church age shall be better than the beginning."

Yet one more time He spoke, asking, "John, did not I save the best wine for last at the wedding of

Cana" (John 2:1–11)? Wine speaks of His tangible presence in Scripture.

Later He showed me the scripture verse that cemented it for me in my heart. Isaiah, chapter 30, tells how God's people would seek to strengthen themselves in the strength of Egypt (the world's system). They would take strength in the idols pursued by the world. Then God would have to bring the people through adversity and affliction for purification. In this process, they would put away their idols and turn their hearts completely back to God. Once this happened God said:

> Then He will give the rain for your seed.
> —Isaiah 30:23

Isaiah is not speaking of natural rain but rather the rain of God's Spirit as described by Joel, Peter and James. Look at what Isaiah goes on to say:

> The [light of the] sun will be seven times brighter—like the light of seven days! So it will be when the Lord begins to heal his people and cure the wounds he gave them.
> —Isaiah 30:26, NLT

The natural sun does not shine seven times

brighter when it is raining. No, God is describing the glory of His Son whom the Scriptures call "the Sun of Righteousness" (Mal. 4:2). His glory will be seven times greater in the days just before His Second Coming.

The latter rain of God's glory will not only bring refreshing to God's people but also to those around them. I have gone to great meetings where God was moving and where there were thousands in attendance each night. Though well attended by the saints, backsliders and sinners, these meetings often did not even put a dent in the surrounding city. As I drove to the services, I wondered when the entire city would be affected. As wonderful as our meetings are, I still watch for the latter rain.

The latter rain is different from past revivals. These revivals affected a city or a region here or there, such as Azusa and Wales. They also affected the nations, but you had to go there to be a part of it. But in the Book of Acts His glory manifested everywhere His disciples went. The glory of God was poured out all over the known world. The latter rain will be poured out all over the earth in a much greater measure!

It is with excitement that I declare, Where we have been and where we are now *is not where we are headed!* We must raise our eyes to the horizon and look for His coming glory!

Adapted from *The Fear of the Lord*, 110–112.

If you are enjoying the Inner Strength Series by
John Bevere, here are some other titles from
Charisma House that we think will minister to you…

Breaking Intimidation
**Break free from the fear
of man**
John Bevere
ISBN: 0-88419-387-X
Retail Price: $13.99

The Bait of Satan
**Don't let resentment
cripple you**
John Bevere
ISBN: 0-88419-374-8
Price: $13.99

Thus Saith the Lord?
**How prophetic excesses
have hurt the church**
John Bevere
ISBN: 0-88419-575-9
Retail Price: $12.99

The Devil's Door
**Recognize the trap of
rebellion**
John Bevere
ISBN: 0-88419-442-6
Price: $12.99

Pathway to His Presence
**A 40-day devotional
leading into His presence**
John and Lisa Bevere
ISBN: 0-88419-654-2
Price: $16.99

The Fear of the Lord
**Gain a holy fear and awe
of God**
John Bevere
ISBN: 0-88419-486-8
Price: $12.99

To pick up a copy of any of these titles, contact your local Christian bookstore or order
online at www.charismawarehouse.com.

I don't think.
I just do as she asks.
Once I strip off my T-shirt,
she pushes me gently
so I'm facedown on the chair.

Her fingers begin at the base of my neck
and work down my spine.

> "Close your eyes
> and open your mind."

Her palms push into my back.

> "Picture in your mind's eye
> a slow moving river, thick and golden."

She rubs my temples.

> "You're under the thick water,
> in a river of honey."

Her hands trace every vertebrae.

> "Breathe in through your skin.
> Let all your breath out and
> allow yourself to fall."

She grasps my shoulders,
then my arms,
then my hands.

"Your bones are heavy.
Your spirit is weighted.
Hold on to the ground
and let your soul rise."

There's a tingling down my back.
Not a chill. More like static electricity.
Little flecks of silver enter
my peripheral vision.
They float and circle,
then pop like bubbles.

I've lost contact with Shasten's hands.
I barely hear her voice.

I'm so concentrated on the
silver flecks, I don't even notice
her hands have stopped.

"William?
You can open your eyes now."

I open my eyes.
The silver flecks
are still there.
As I take in the night sky above us,
they start to fade away

"How do you feel?"

"Wow.
That
was
amazing."

I put my T-shirt on.
"I saw some things.
Little silver things.
Almost like flames."

       "That's it.
       That's the energy."

Touch

Jill Archer's out
all week at
a conference so
I spend first period
studying.

I keep thinking about Patches.
Where he is.
How he is.

Coach has me watch
some videos of football plays
instead of working out with
the class.

I'm pretty amped up
by the time Bio starts.

Ollie's early as usual,
but Shasten's late.
Very late.

Mr. Lipston's already started his lecture
when she serpentines through the door.

He nods at her,
marks something in his notebook,
and keeps talking.

"Hey, thought you were out sick."

> "No, I had to take my mum
> to the doctor."

"Is it serious?"

"That depends.
It's a scheduled appointment,
but if she missed it,
she'd probably die."

"That sounds more than serious.
Sorry."

"What's Lipston excited about today?"

"Shhhh," Ollie whispers.
"We're learning all the
types of cells in the brain."

"Gray ones, you *brain*iac?"

"Funny.
Listen up. It's really interesting!"

Shasten's really quiet.
I want to ask her
about Whole-Is-Tech,
but she doesn't seem to be
in a talking mood.

She also seems sad.

I wish I could cheer her up,
but I don't want to come off
flippant.

I rack all the cells in my brain,
but I can't find the right words.

When Gramps was
first hospitalized,
I was afraid to touch him.

But even though he was unconscious,
I always hugged him
good-bye after each visit.

When Gramps
finally woke up,
he said he'd felt me
hug him.
He said, "There's a lot of
healing in your touch."

Huh. Didn't remember that
until just now.

Since I can't find
the right words,
maybe I'll try out a touch.

Maybe.

Mr. Lipston has us set up
our microscopes to look at
slides of brain tissue of a frog.

I angle my chair nearer to Shasten,
but she turns away
as I reach for her arm.

I step closer as
she turns back.

Ouch!
My chin slams into
her forehead.

"Shit, sorry," I whisper.
She's holding her forehead.
I'm holding my chin.

I give up on the
entire touch strategy.

But then
her hand's
on my arm.

She's leaning into
my chest,
putting her head
on my shoulder.

"Thank you."

She shudders against me.

I pull her
at her slim waist
and bring her closer.

There's sincerity
in this touch.

I can almost hear
her thoughts.

"You're supposed to be
studying the brain cells,
not each other."

"You're right, Ollie."
Shasten pulls away.

Talk about moving energy.

*Penguins, penguins, penguins
on an iceberg . . .*

Cheeseburger

I plop down next to Ollie
under the tree
as soon as Stats lets out.

"So are you two an item now?"

"What? Who?"

"You and Mr. Lipston, dude."
Ollie groans.
"You and Shasten of course."

"Us? No.
I think she likes me, though."

"Yeah."

I open my backpack.
The usual:
SPAM, mustard,
and mayo sandwich,
a hard-boiled egg,
and saltines.

I'm wondering what to eat first
when a shadow falls over us.

"Here. You need this now
so you'll have energy for later."

Coach drops a greasy paper bag in my lap.
It's hot and smells awesome.
I rip it open:
cheeseburger and fries.

"Excellent. Thanks, Coach."
Coach mock-salutes,
then jogs off toward the playing fields.

"Why'd he give you that?"

"I'm trying out
for the football team today."

"*What*?
No, no, no.
You *can't* do that."

"What's your problem?
Why not?"

"You just can't, that's all."

Ollie slams his plastic food container
on the ground.

"Hey, Ollie.
Calm down.
Tell me what's wrong, okay?"

"You're already on your way
with Shasten. If you try out
for the football team, well,
you'll probably be good."

"So . . . that's bad?"

"Yes, very bad.
You said this was *our* thing."

"What? Our lunch tree?
Yeah, it's our thing."

"So, if you make the team,
you'll be hanging out with them."
Ollie points toward the plaza.
"Having lunch with them and everything."

I look over and see
Needlemier, Bender,
and the other meatheads
dominating the center tables
like royalty.

"I don't see that happening."

"It will, trust me."

"But they're dickwads."

"You say that now,
but you'll change your mind
and I'll have invested all this
time with you and end up all alone."

I can kind of see
where Ollie's coming from.
Friends are hard for him
to come by.

But it's not like
we have anything
in common other than
Bio class.

Does he really
expect me to
hang with him
forever?

It's not like we made
a sacred vow
or some crazy thing.

But maybe to Ollie
we did.

"Maybe I'll suck."

Ollie chipmunk-chitters.

"Yeah. Maybe you will."

He tries to nudge me
with his elbow, but misses.

Tryouts

I'm a total outsider
on the football field.

Seems like everyone knows each other.
Even the freshmen know who's who
more than I do.

Coach calls everyone
into a large huddle.

He talks about "team,"
but I tune out.

I glance at all the
guys around me.

Each one seems to have
a different level of anxiety.
Each one a different desire.
A different reason to be here.

My eyes fall on Needlemier.
He's watching me,
and it makes me uneasy.
Maybe he's trying to psych me out,
but I sense a darker intention
than just football.

We warm up, stretch,
and then the running starts.
Sprints from midfield.

Coach is trying to find
his fastest guys.
The sprints quickly
become a competition.

We sprint from the forty-yard line.
The first to cross the goal line moves on.
The process of elimination is quick.

The final four with the best times
are Needlemier, Jim,
some skinny freshman
named Teddy,
and me.

Coach keeps timing us
with his stopwatch,
but he's not saying
who's the fastest.

Next up is the skills part: passing and catching.

     "Ten and out,"
     Coach says.

Jim runs and catches.
Then Teddy.
My turn.

The ball's snapped.
I run to the target spot,
but the ball's way behind me.

     "Flash, you're running a slant,"
     Coach calls. "Cut to the outside."

The ball's snapped again.
I run ten yards, then cut to the right.
The ball's in my hands before I realize it.

We go through different routes.
Jim helps me learn them.

I'm catching okay
until we switch
quarterbacks.

Now the ball's either
just out of my reach
or behind me.

Of course the new quarterback's
Needlemier.

>"He sucks, Coach," Needlemier whines.
>"He hasn't caught half my passes."

Should I tell Coach Needlemier's
sandbagging me?
I don't want to be a whiner like him,
but I don't want Coach to think I suck either.

>"Switch, guys."

>"What? Why, Coach?"

>"No whining, Needlemier. Let's go."

Ha!
My turn to pass.
I consider leading him too far,
but what would that do?

If Coach is trying to judge my skills,
I'll just have to focus on doing my best.

The ball's snapped.
I drop back, set my foot,
and launch a rocket
toward the right sideline
just as Needlemier cuts.
It's a perfect throw and catch.

> "Good. Okay now,
> gimme a Go pattern."

"A what?"

> "Long pass.
> Just like you did in class to Jim."

"Okay."
I nod at Jim.
"Goal line, right side."

Jim lines up wide.
I get the ball
and drop back.

Jim's going flat out.

I set my back foot
and then transfer all my weight
forward like a whip.

The football rockets
from my hand
and climbs high.

Jim gets under it.

Touchdown!

There's a rumble through the guys.
Guys I've never met
are patting me on the back.

I look over at Needlemier.
He's not happy.

A Good Hit

"Everyone has to hit,"
Coach directs.

We line up in pairs.

Coach stands on a tackle sled
with padded tackle dummies
attached in front
like shields.

The assistant coach blows the whistle
and we launch ourselves.

Bender hits the tackle dummy square,
driving his side of the sled back a foot.

Needlemier hits the dummy with little effect.

"Got any pointers, Jimbo?"

"Plant both feet, then shoot forward."

"You don't belong here,"
Needlemier whispers at me.

He pisses me off.
Not just the barbs he throws,
but his goddamned arrogance.

I'm trying to think of a good comeback
when the whistle blows.
I lunge blindly at the tackle dummy,
but make solid contact.

I drive forward
and knock Coach
clear off the sled.

Needlemier laughs.

Coach picks himself up.

    "Now *that's* how you hit, gentlemen."

Needlemier stops laughing.

Dinner for Twenty

My feet don't seem
to touch the ground
on my walk home.

Although, as I see my reflection
in a window,
I'm not really walking.
I'm strutting.

"Now that's how you hit, gentlemen,"
I say to myself
as I reach the next set of windows.

I'm so glad Coach gave me
that cheeseburger and fries.
SPAM just wouldn't have gotten me
through tryouts.
And right now, I'm ravenous.

My night off
before two nights on.

I hope Dad's got something for dinner.
I hope he's not mad I'm so late.
I hope he doesn't ask for an explanation.
Guess I could tell him I was working.

After that Hail Mary pass to Jim,
maybe Coach'll replace Needlemier
with me as quarterback.

I'm faster and I can throw farther.
I think I'm Coach's favorite.
Plus I might possibly be
prettier.

No, I have to admit,
actually Needlemier is
good-looking.
If you like fine, angular features.

When I get home
and dump my stuff,
I find the note in the kitchen.
There's a
twenty-dollar bill
attached to it:

> **Game night out.**
> **Get a pizza.**

Crying

The nearest pizza place
is Hiro's Pies.
This place serves pizza
and sushi.

Weird.

I've never had sushi,
and I'm not sure
I want to.

I walk past the sushi bar
and gaze at the array of
raw fish.

A woman at the bar's eating
a deep-fried shrimp
with the eyes and legs
still attached.

Gross.

I'm a
hand-tossed-
pepperoni-
with-extra-
cheese guy.

Add a Coke,
insert ear buds,
and I'm "a hog in mud,"
as G'ma would say.

While I'm waiting for my order,
I start my alternative radio playlist
and fall deep inside my head.

I start a nice
daydream about Shasten,
which gets rudely interrupted
when my pizza's ready.

Without much effort,
I polish off
four slices
and three refills
of Coke.

I finish dinner
with a dish of soft serve
and a gut-relieving burp.

I'm suddenly aware
that everyone around me's
heard it.

"Uh . . . sorry."

I pay and get back
two bucks
even after a tip.

I take a shortcut home,
down a long alley.

My phone beeps
the battery death tone, so
I pull my ear buds out.

I look up the alley
and see a dog
about three houses ahead.

It's not moving.
It's just watching me.

The streetlight
behind it is
blacking out any color
or features.

Could it be
the blue-eyed dog?

"Hey, boy."

I approach slowly
and hold out my hand
as if I've got a snack.
I'm within ten feet of him
when he bolts away.
It's him. It's the blue-eyed dog.

"Hey, wait!"

The dog hops into a yard
through a gap in
a wooden fence.

I peek in at the dark backyard.
The house is old, sort of run-down.
The grass is tall, brown in spots.

Does the dog live here?
If he does,
I'll be able to find him easily now.

There's an ugly, stained,
neon-yellow sofa
leaning against an outer wall.

A beat-up scooter
and a plastic tricycle
in the shape of a pony
are lying in the grass.

I don't see any water bowls
or doggie toys.

The wind gusts,
blowing a faint whistling
through the trees.

Or is it?

As I listen, the whistle changes.
It loses its breath and becomes more solid,
more distinct, more alarming.
It's a faint shrill cry.

Not a baby's cry.
Not a dog or a cat.
It's a kid.

I fit myself through the gap
the dog went through,
and I'm inside the fenced yard.

The cries are definitely
coming from the house.

I move closer.

The cries seem to be
coming from below ground.
But how is that possible?

I walk around the back of the house.
There's an open window below the deck
above a flowerbed.

A soft light glows inside the room.
The cries grow louder.
I can't see anyone inside,
only shadows flickering against the walls.

Between the cries, I start to hear
a man's heavy breathing.
A man's grunts.

          "It hurts,"
          a kid's voice says.

Patches?!

"Stop!" I yell.
"Stop! Now!"

The crying stops.
More lights come on.
Heavy footsteps approach.

My phone's dead,
so I can't call the cops.
I don't know what else to do,
so I run across the yard and
out through the gap in the fence.

There's nowhere to hide in the alley
except behind a trash bin.

If they come after me,
I'll just have to confront them.
Maybe if I make enough noise,
someone will hear and call the cops.

I hold my breath.

At least I've located Patches.
At least the assholes hurting him
know someone's seen them now.
That someone knows.

Maybe that's all it'll take.
Maybe they'll stop.
They've got to stop.

Leviathans

A storm's raging outside.
Ice is hammering against
the windows.
It's impossible
to sleep.

I get out of bed
and throw on a jacket
over my T-shirt and boxers.

There are screams in the wind.

I run outside into the sleet,
toward the screams.

I struggle against the wind,
following a path up a sand dune.
I stumble to the top and
see the source of the screams.

In the churning surf,
huge whales are undulating
and thrashing like sea serpents.
They're trapped
on the sand.

Their blowholes steam
with hot vapor.

Their screams
are shaking in my chest.

People are running into
the breakers to help the animals.

I rush out to join them,
but stop as I hit the freezing water.

Instead of trying to save the whales,
these people are stabbing them
with their hands!

"Stop!" I shout.
But the wind carries my voice away.

They've shaped their hands
like scythes and are driving them
into the whales' sides.

Blood's flowing like rivers
from the slashes
in their ruined bodies.

I grab the nearest man,
pull him around
to face me.

But he's got no eyes,
no nose,
no mouth.
No face at all.

None of these people
have faces.

A whale bellows
in pain.
It rolls,
trying to get away
from the faceless people.

It's going to roll
over on top
of me.

Air Vent

I wake up
as I hit the cold linoleum.

It takes me a second
to realize I've been dreaming.

I remember running home
from that horrible house
and trying to do
my Creative Writing
homework.

I was supposed to
read the first chapter
of *Moby Dick*,
then write about
Ishmael's
character traits.
Big snore.
I guess I fell asleep.

I'm wide awake now,
so I get up.
May as well finish my homework.

But as I look
through my notebook,
I see I've already
finished all of it.

The sun's just up,
and the sky's clear.

I get dressed.
I've got to go back to that house.
I jog down to the alley.

If I can get some sort
of evidence,
some little bit of proof,
maybe I can save Patches.

It doesn't take long
to find the gap in the
wooden fence.

I peek in.

Nothing seems to have changed.
No dog.
No sounds of life.
No sounds of someone making breakfast,
or showering,
or watching the news.
But most important of all,
no cries.

I slip into the yard,
move around to the back deck.

Something's different.

Something's wrong.
Very wrong.

There's no open window
under the deck above a flowerbed.
There's no flowerbed at all.
There's no window at all.
Just an air vent.

They must've
covered up the window
as soon as I left last night.
But how?

I pull on the vent,
try to wedge it off the side of the house,
but it's securely bolted to the wall.

What the hell is going on?

I glance around.
The stained sofa's still leaning against the wall.
The scooter and pony-shaped tricycle
are still lying in the grass.

There's got to be
another window.
It was dark.
I could be remembering
things wrong.

I walk around the house.
But there aren't any windows set low near the deck.

When I get round to the front of the house,
I realize why there are no signs of life.

The front wall of the house
is completely missing.
Gone.
The bricks of the front wall are black.
The windows are all broken out.

This house got burned out
a long time ago.
The blue-eyed dog doesn't live here.
Patches doesn't live here.

No one lives here.

Off Balance

Am I standing straight?
Maybe my up is actually sideways.
Is my north pointing west?

I *know* I saw that dog.
The house is real.
But now I'm not sure about what I saw
through the window.
Not anymore.

Maybe what I saw was a vision.
Maybe I *am* an empath.
Regardless, it's psycho fucking madness.

Roster

There's a mob
at the front of the locker room.

"What's going on?"

>"Coach just posted
>the roster.
>Come on!"

Jim and I push to the front of the crowd.
The roster's divided between
offense and defense.
If your name isn't there,
then you didn't make the cut.

>"Yes!" Jim pumps the air.
>"Wide receiver. Awesome."

I look down the offense list.
I find the quarterback position:
Needlemier.
Damn.

I don't see my name anywhere.
WTF?

I have a stronger arm
and I'm faster
than Needlemier.
What's Coach thinking?

I scan the offense list again.
I didn't even make the team.

"Defense, huh? Loser."
Needlemier bumps me.

Defense?
What?

I turn back to the roster,
scan the defense list.

There I am.
Safety: Stout

Coach comes out of his office
and hands slips of paper to all of us.

"Flash, I need this release signed
by your dad so you can play."

I take the paper
without looking at it.
I guess my face
has "disappointed"
written across it
in neon.

"Look, I put you as safety because
with your speed you'll close the gaps.
Plus, you hit like a bull."

"Yeah, thanks.
I get it.
Just, I was hoping for offense."

"Yeah, I know. You do have a good arm,
but Needlemier knows the playbook already."

"I could learn the plays."

"I know you could.
But here's the thing—
our defense is weak;
you'll make us stronger."

"I get it."
I'm all in for the team.

Lowest Common Denominator

"So how's your job, son?"

"It's okay.
I have to go later today.
It's work, but it pays."

"Sounds like a job alright."

I pour myself a bowl of cereal,
then slide the permission slip
across the table.
"Will you sign this?"

"Hang on, Sport.
Give me a moment
to get chemically balanced."

I watch him
out of the corner of my eye
as he pours his coffee.

He opens the oven,
removes a bottle,
and adds some bourbon
to the steaming mug.

"So, now, what's this?"

"Permission slip.
Need your signature to play."

"Play what?"

"Football."

Dad puts on his reading glasses
and studies the paper.
His eyebrows knit together.

"This reads like
you've already
made the team."

"Well, yeah. I have."

"So you tried out and didn't tell me?"

"I didn't want to say anything.
Ya know?
If I didn't make the cut."

He cocks his head and nods,
as if he's weighing
the amount of truth
in my words.

"What position?"

"Safety."

"That's a tough position.
Gotta be smart.
I could give you some pointers."

"That'd be great."
I hope that'll be
the only cost
for his signature.

"But . . . hold on. Hold on."

What now?

He flips the release over.
He draws a small circle
in the middle of the page.
Then he draws
five smaller circles
to surround the first.

He fills in the outer circles
with frowning faces.
He draws a smiley face
in the middle circle.

His own face contorts
as he shifts in his chair.

He must be mad.
He's going to deny me
for not asking him
if I could try out.

      "Tell me something . . .
      who farted?"

I look at him,
then at the paper
and back again.

Then I burst out laughing
as it hits me.

Not his silly sketch humor
but the rank,
onions-and-rotten-egg scent
of Dad's flatulence.

The smell must be
more than even he expected.
He starts gagging and fanning the air
with the permission slip.
We both laugh—hard.
With every laugh, we smell more fart.

Finally, we both get up
and stumble into the TV room.

Dad takes a deep breath,
then runs back into the kitchen
like the room's on fire.

He emerges, still holding his breath,
then doubles over, gasping.

I'm afraid he's
having an attack
of some sort.

But he's just joking.
He straightens up
and hands me the release,
complete with his flowing script of a signature.

It's sort of telling that before tonight,
we hardly ever talked,
and never did anything together.

He's my father, so I have his blood.
But even so,
we can't be much further apart.

Something so simple,
we connected over a stupid fart?

This might be the first time
Dad and I have ever laughed together.

I may eventually forget that nasty smell,
but I doubt I'll ever forget the laughing.

Mr. Popular

Coach was right.
Making the football team
does change things.

Everyone seems to be
looking at me differently.
People I've never met
seem to know my name now.

Guys pat me on the back
or fist bump
or give me a bro nod.

It's like being part of a secret club.

I can tell the girls are more interested.
I overheard one of them
asking Pete about me.

This morning I get a text
from Shasten
that she has to
take her little brother
to the doctor.

I make sure to take better
notes in Bio with neater
handwriting. Just in case
Shasten wants to see them.

If she's smart, she'll ask Ollie for his notes.
If she asks me, she likes me.

Family Portrait

Mrs. Long has us writing
about our families today.

I get a good set of paragraphs
about Gramps and G'ma.
I write about Dad's
weird sense of humor
and his obsession with sports.

But I have no idea
what to write about my mother.

Do I write that she's a
Sports Illustrated photographer?

Do I write she works at the White House?

Do I write she's dead?

The bell rings.

Thing You Own

I'm heading through the plaza
when I'm stopped by
Brinlee Wilcox Thomas.

She's the head cheerleader
and damn hot.

"So you're the new guy."

"Yup, I'm William."

"I'm having a party
next week to kick off the
season. You should come."

"Great. I'll plan on it."

"Good deal. Nice to meet you."

I wave as she turns away,
her perfect blond ponytail swishing.

"Hey, *Flash*."

Since when does Needlemier call me that?
I nod at him.

He's sitting on top
of the middle table
like it's his throne.

"So what's the deal with you
and Roly Poly Ollie?"

"We study together.
He's wicked smaht."

      Needlemier snorts.
      "You know Shasten's mine,
      right?"

"I don't think *she*
sees it that way."

      "Well, she is.
      So you lay off."

My stomach ignites,
and my anger goes
from simmer to boil
in one second flat.

I step toward him.
He slides off the table to meet me.

"I don't see it
that way either."

      "You will."

"You do realize
that people
aren't things
that you own.
Right?"

      "That's where you're wrong.
      I own *you*."

"How'd you figure that?"

      "I'm the captain of the team.
      So what I say goes."

"Is that right?
Well, maybe
it's time that changed."

Needlemier puffs up.
His eyes narrow.
Tough guy,
but I sense something else.
I sense fear.

I see a flicker of an image:
Needlemier's standing alone
in the middle of a crowd.
Afraid.

I walk away,
not so much to avoid a fight,
but because Needlemier's emotions
are making me uneasy.

      "Chicken shit."

If I turn back, I'll have to deck him.
I'm sure I could take him,
but Coach might sideline me,
or worse, kick me off the team.

I get over to the tree
just as Ollie's finishing his lunch.

"Sorry I'm late."

    "You're only late
    if you intended to be here."

"What does that even *mean*?"

    "Lunch is almost over."

"I'm here now."

    "Yeah. But I saw you with them.
    That's how it all starts."

"Ollie, really?
I like you, I do,
but you don't own me."

I don't mean for my anger at Needlemier
to spill over onto Ollie.
My words are too harsh.
My voice too loud.
My manner too rough.

Something in Ollie's eyes changes.

He's stung,
and I'm the hornet.
His finger's slammed,
and I'm the door.

I hurt him.
Damn.

He rushes off without a word.

I don't follow him.

"Hey, Flash," Coach calls.
"You got that release for me?"

"What?
Oh, yeah.
Here ya go."

I pull out the crumpled release
from my backpack
and hand it to him.

"Perfect. Now here's the uniform,
shoes, and equipment list."

He hands me a sheet
with a list of stores,
equipment, and prices.

Shit.
Making the football team
is going
to cost.

Sunset

"Zillah, I'm sorry, but
I'm not going to be able
to work Friday nights."

> "I know. It's okay.
> Coach told me.
> Congrats on making the team."

I'm happy to tell
everyone I meet
that I made
the football team.

I even text J-Bob.

He says I'm a total sellout,
but I know he thinks it's cool.

I rush through two loads of
Whole-Is-Tech laundry
and finish early.

I enter the solarium,
hoping Shasten will be there.
But except for a couple
meditating on the floor,
the place is empty.

It's not the end of the world,
but I want to share my good news
with her.

I set about refilling the incense burners,
when I see her doing her homework
at the edge of the solarium.

"Nice place to do homework."

"Oh, hi, William.
Yeah, it is."

"So I've got news.
I made the football team."

"Really? That's great.
Although . . . you and Bradley
on the same team . . . ?"

"It's okay.
I'm on defense.
So if we lose,
it'll be all his fault."

We laugh.

Shasten's laugh's like
wind chimes and birdsong.
She's so adorable.
Even her love of wearing
mismatched knee highs
is cool.

"I want to show you something!"

She hops up and drags me
to the edge of the roof.

"Look at the sunset!"

From up here,
we can see
the shops that run
along the street,
the beach,
and the ocean.

California sunsets
are amazing.

In Kansas the sun drops behind a hill
and that's about it.

Here you can see the sun
for miles and miles and miles
over the ocean.

It's so beautiful I expect to hear
a hiss when the sun
finally disappears in the sea.

Shasten leans into me,
her hand warm on my arm.

She looks up at me
and leans closer.

I think she wants to kiss me.

I know I want to kiss her.

I pull her closer.

Suddenly,
I see a flash of red
down below us.

A familiar giggle carries up to the roof.
I push Shasten away
and rush to the edge.

"Hey?"

"Patches?!"

And there he is,
running down the sidewalk
toward the beach.

"What's wrong?"

"That kid!
Down there.
See him?"
I point.
"He's running toward the beach."

Shasten peers down from the roof.

"I guess.
Why?
Who is he?"

"His name's Patches.
I think he's in trouble and—"

"I feel something wrong."

"Exactly. He's being abused."

Explanation

I explain to Shasten
how I keep seeing
Patches alone on the street.
How I followed him into a house and
how Patches told me about his abuse.

"And then the other night,
I think I heard him crying
and saw him being abused
through a window in an old house.
But I must be going nuts
because when I went back
to the house the next day,
the whole house was
totally burned out.
No one lives there!"

Shasten closes her eyes
and sways side to side,
like a willow in a breeze.
She looks so thoughtful and peaceful,
I don't dare interrupt her.

Finally she opens her eyes.

      "You have a very strong link
      to that little boy.
      I can sense it.
      I think that's why you can see
      what's happening to him."

"But I didn't see, not really.
Like I said, the house is burned out,
there wasn't any window,
only an air vent."

"You did see it, William.
Just not through your eyes.
You saw it happen through *his*."

WTF.
Her words knock the air out of me.
As I slowly comprehend what she's
trying to say, I feel lightheaded
and I've got to sit down.
I sink to the floor.

"So you don't think I'm crazy?"

"No, not at all.
You're not crazy, and you're not a liar.
I know you saw something
and heard something.
It's real for you."

"So the shadows on the wall . . .
a man breathing . . .
the kid crying . . .
You're saying I experienced all that
through Patches?"

"I think so.
That's the only explanation
that makes sense."

"I guess that *does* sort of make sense.
In an incense burning–
crack smoking–
ancient aliens
sort of way."

"You saw the energy when
I worked on you, William.
Remember?"

"Yeah."

"This isn't crazy,
but it's also not explainable
by science or anything."

"It doesn't seem real."

"There's no ancient book
and no old dude in robes
telling you how to worship
God, but is this any less real?
I believe this is real
because this is how it works
for me."

"Sorry. This is all new to me.
A totally new way of thinking."

"I get that." Shasten
sits down next to me.
"It's okay."

"I wouldn't believe any of this,
you know, except I'm the one
experiencing it firsthand.
And I'm convinced there's a kid
out there who needs help—fast."

Shasten slips her arms around me.

"I'll help you
figure this out.
Let me be your guide."

Strategy

Shasten and I strategize
how we're going to find Patches.

I want to watch Buckaroo Preschool.
But Shasten thinks the only way
I'll find him is by our telepathic link.

> "You don't even know his real name.
> I mean, who names their kid Patches?
> Has he ever mentioned his last name?"

"Well, no."

> "So what are you going to search with?"

"But I've seen him
at the preschool—twice."

> "You've also seen him
> in a burned-out building."

"Yeah, there's that."

> "You need to meditate on him,
> open up that link,
> see what he sees,
> hear his voice again,
> and maybe you'll get a clue
> where to find him."

"*Meditate* on him?
How do I do that?"

"Just sit here
and empty your mind."

Shasten lights some incense
in a bowl on a table nearby.

"The objective is to
become aware of the present.
Don't think of future possibilities
or past events."

At this point,
all I can think about is her.

"Start with your breathing."

Focus, Stout.
My mind shifts,
slowly shifts.

"Breathe in through your nose.
Now pause.
Exhale through your mouth.
Pause again.
Repeat.
Now count each exhale."

I do as she guides, but
I lose count after the tenth breath.
I lose focus of the room
and become more and more aware
of me.

"Focus on a singular
piece of your body.
A toe or a finger
or a strand of your hair."

It's weird,
but I get what she's saying.
I can actually sense
a single strand of hair
on my head.

"Keep breathing.
Keep focusing.
Now, start to see
where Patches is."

I look through my closed eyes
and search the blackness
of my mind.

I begin to see something,
a room of some sort.

"Shasten, I think I've got him."

"Keep breathing."
She squeezes my hand.
"Tell me what you see."

"He's there, in the corner
of a big room.
I see potted plants.
There's a sofa and chairs.
In front of the sofa's
a low table with something on it.
I think it's a candle—no, incense."

"Very funny, William."

"I can feel him.
Really, I can feel him."

Shasten smacks me
on the back of my head.

"If you're not going to take
me seriously, I'm going to go."

I open my eyes.
In front of us is the bowl of incense
on the table, in front of the sofa,
and potted trees.

"I really thought
I was linked.
I could feel him."

Shasten gets up and
storms out in a huff.

"Hey, wait!
I wasn't joking—
I really thought I was getting it.
I'm sorry."

Mr. Billings

I get down to the front door just in time
to see the taillights of
Shasten's car disappearing.
Shit.

I check the clock.
It's closing time.

Zillah's already gone,
so I lock up
and decide to do
a last check of the
rooms.

To my surprise there's a man
lying on the massage table.

As far as I can tell, he's not wearing
anything except a towel.

"Um. Hello?"

>"Yeah, hi.
>I was afraid
>they forgot about me."

"I think they might've."

>"It's okay. You're here now."

"But I'm not . . ."

      "My regular masseuse, yeah I know.
      My neck is just killing me, though,
      so whatever you do will be
      an improvement."

"Um, we're actually closed now."

      "Oh, right. There's an extra hundred
      on the counter to cover your overtime."

I don't know what to do,
but walking away from
one hundred dollars cash
goes against my religion.

Especially when I've got to
pay for a football uniform,
shoes, and pads.

I mean how hard can this be?

"Okay, sir."

      "Call me Steve. Steve Billings."

"Okay, Mr. Billings,
nice to meet you.
Now, close your eyes
and clear your mind."

I'm trying to copy exactly
what Shasten did for me
the other night.

I start massaging his back,
then move down.
My fingers trace
each of his vertebrae.

I push my palms into his back,
as I move up.

Mr. Billings moans.

"Let's start with your breathing.
Inhale through your nose
and hold it.
Exhale through your mouth."

Mr. Billings lets out a chest full of air.

"Let yourself go.
Picture yourself underwater,
in an ocean of honey."

Billings groans.

"Do you feel the waves?
Don't swim.
Let the waves take you."

Billings begins to make odd noises.
I don't sense he's in pain.
I sense he's surprised.

I start massaging his head.

Billings groans again.

"Am I hurting you?"

       "No, no. Not at all."

I wish he'd tell me to stop,
because I really have to call
Shasten.

I finish by massaging his temples.
An image flashes in my mind:
A car.
A crash.
An airbag deploying.
A shattered window.

I shake my head and
check the clock.
It's been over forty-five minutes.
How'd that happen?

"I think we're done.
How are you feeling?"

Billings doesn't move.
Maybe he's fallen asleep.

"I'll let you get dressed now, okay?"

I rush out
to the men's room
and wash my hands.

I give Billings a few minutes
to get dressed,
then return to clean up.

Room 2's empty.

Mr. Billings has vanished,
along with my one hundred dollars.
Figures.

Text-pology

I locate Shasten's cell number
from the directory at the spa
and key in a text.

I'M SO SORRY
I DO TAKE YOU SERIOUSLY
REALLY

I wait for what seems like forever.
Then my phone buzzes.

NOT ANGRY
I HAD TO GO. MY AUNT
WAS WAITING

I REALLY THOUGHT
I WAS LINKED TO HIM

IT WAS YOUR FIRST ATTEMPT
TRY AGAIN

I WILL

REMEMBER WHAT I SHOWED YOU

I WILL
HEY I DID MY FIRST MASSAGE

WHAT DO YOU MEAN?

SOME GUY WAS IN ROOM 2

OMG! MR. BILLINGS!
I FORGOT ABOUT HIM!

DON'T WORRY
I TOOK CARE OF HIM

THANKS
YOU SAVED ME
I <3 U

Freeze-frame me.

I <3 U
I heart you.

Technically
"heart" translates to "love,"
but if she were saying
"heart" out loud, that doesn't
quite mean "love."

Does she mean
I love you or
I heart you?

I just might be driving myself crazy.
I guess I should be happy
that she even feels something
more than "I like you as a friend."

Unless . . .
that's what I <3 U means.

I AM driving myself crazy.

Feels Good

Life is great and getting even better.

I just made the football team,
I've got a job,
Dad and I are getting along,
and I think I have a new girlfriend.

Girlfriend.

Shasten is so damn amazing.

Beautiful, sexy, smart, witty.

And she knows shit.
Strange shit,
but she knows it well.

She's my spiritual guide.
My angel.
As long as I don't fuck things up.

Angels.

I have so many.
Shasten,
Coach,
Jill Archer,
Ollie.
Even Dad in his own way.
He's not around much,
with work and watching sports,
but maybe that's good.

Good.

Life feels good.
How could I know
when I left Kansas
that my life would
feel so good?

Short from Now On

I get to school early,
which I've never done before.

But I like school,
which I've never felt before.

I take a seat in Jill Archer's wooden chair.
It's not so uncomfortable today.

Jill Archer's excited to see me,
or maybe she's just had too much coffee.

She moves quickly,
almost leaping into her chair.

"How was your conference?"

  "Amazing. I really learned a lot.
  How have things been here
  with you?"

"Life is great."

  "Wow. How so?"

"I made the football team,
and I think I have a girlfriend."

  "Well, all of that is indeed
  ingredients for feeling good.
  How are your grades?"

"Pretty good I think.
Maybe one B,
maybe two."

     "Not bad.
     Anything *troubling* you?"

I thought I'd start telling her about
Needlemier,
but something else pops out of my mouth.
"Well, now that you ask,
there's this dog
I keep seeing.
He's got blue eyes.
I've never seen a dog
with such blue eyes.
I'm worried about him."

     "Why is that?"

"I think he's a stray.
No collar or anything.
He keeps running away,
but I get a sense he wants
to be found."

     "This is very interesting, William.
     This tells me a lot about you."

"That I like dogs?"

     "Yes, but also that you care."

"Caring's good, though,
right?"

"It's a very good sign."

"So do I still need counseling?"

"You still have to meet with me, yes.
But we can keep the meetings short
from now on."

"Cool.
I mean, not that I don't like
being here."

"I understand."

There's a knock on her door.

Her face screws up.
She's not happy
with the interruption.

She opens the door
and reveals
two uniformed cops.

"Goodness.
Can I help you officers?"

"Jill Archer?
You're the school counselor?"

"Yes, I'm in a session right now."

"We've had a complaint about a boy,
possibly a student here.
Seems he's been seen stalking
preschool kids."

The cops look past Jill at me,
and my core temperature
drops below zero.

Stay calm.

"William,
I think we're done for today.
See you tomorrow, okay?"

"What?
Yeah, sure.
Okay."

I get up and walk by the cops.

They stare holes
through me
as I pass them.

Suddenly my life doesn't feel so good.

Paranoia

I'm on edge all morning,
fully expecting the cops
to show up in Bio.

I imagine being pointed at,
pulled out, and handcuffed.

I'm so distracted, I hardly notice
that Ollie isn't talking to me.

Shasten's busy catching up
on last night's homework.

> "I didn't get my homework done
> because I was doing online searches
> for any kid named Patches."

"You were?
Did you find anything?"

> "Nothing. Maybe we can go over
> to that preschool later."

"Um. No. I don't think
that's a good idea."

> "Are you okay?
> You don't seem all here."

"I'm not.
I can't tell you all the details,
but it's important for me
to find that kid.
Extremely important."

Ollie-ology

The bell rings.
Ollie's quick to exit.

I wait to exit
when the throng's
the largest.

I figure I can hide from
the cops easier in a herd.

I slip around a corner
and survey the hallways.

The two cops are in front of the
admin building.

They keep their eyes on the flow
of kids, but they don't seem keen
on any single type or anyone in
particular.

I move through the plaza.
The center table's void of
Needlemier and his meatheads.
Wonder where they are.

    "Knock it off!."

I know that voice.
I look over at the lunch tree.

No. No. No!

Needlemier,
Bender,
and the meatheads
have Ollie surrounded.

Ollie's rolled up in a ball
on the grass,
clutching his backpack to his chest.

He's not giving them an active target,
like playing dead for grizzly bears.

A smart strategy,
only,
these aren't bears.

I move quickly, but not too fast.
Don't want to draw attention
before I have to.

As soon as I'm closer,
I yell, "Leave him alone!"

Needlemier smiles, all smug.

"Don't you have some puppy
to kick?"

          "This puppy'll do just fine."

"Just leave him alone."

          "Is this little nobody your friend
          or your lover?"

"I'd rather be a little nobody,
than an evil somebody."
Ollie's voice is muffled by the grass.

I glance over my shoulder,
looking for the cops.
Where the hell are they
when you need them?

"We'll leave, but not before
everyone slaps him once."

"What are you talking about?
No one's slapping anyone."

"Everyone on my team's
slappin' this pansy.
Aren't you part of the team, *Flash*?"

"I am."

"So take a shot.
Take a shot for the team."

Something he says clicks.
I slap my own face—hard.

"What the hell are you doing?"

"I'm taking one for the team,
like you said, *Captain*.
Instead of slapping Ollie,
y'all can slap me."

"The fuck you say?"

"What fun's there in that?"
Bender quips.
"You'll probably like it."

I stand ready.
Needlemier
squares off with me.

"Everything okay here,
gentlemen?"

Our little square dance
has caught the cops' attention.

"All good here, Officer."
Needlemier's voice is scary smooth.
"Just talking football."

I don't look up.
Needlemier and the meatheads
disperse.

The cops march into the parking lot.
They seem to be looking for something
in particular.

"Thanks, William."

"No worries, Ollie.
It pisses me off
when those asshats
interrupt our lunch thing.
You okay?"

"Yeah. Those asshats."

I watch the cops
as they move methodically
from car to car.

The Tip

I've washed and dried
two loads of laundry
by the time Zillah finds me
out back
dumping the trash.

"William, can I see you in my office?"

"Right now? I still have some
folding to do."

"Now would be good, William."

I don't like how she says that.
Her tone seems a little too
serious for a discussion about
organic cleaners or the
proper method to dispose
of incense ashes.

"You go on in," Zillah says
when we get to her office.
"I'll be right there."

I'm surprised
to see Shasten
in Zillah's office already.

"What's going on?"

"I'm not sure, but it's something big.
Zillah had Judy take over the rest
of my appointments tonight."

Freeze-frame me.

Have the cops tracked me to my job?

Zillah's talking to someone
in the lobby.
We hear a man's voice
as they get closer.

> "Mr. Billings, thank you for coming."

"Billings!"

> "Oh, no! He must be pissed
> that I forgot about him
> last night."

"Or maybe I hurt him.
I didn't really know what I was doing."

> "Zillah's going to fire me."
> Shasten's frantic.
> "William, I can't lose this job."

I want to hug her,
but before I can get up,
Zillah and Billings enter the office.

> "Kids, I think you know Mr. Billings."

We nod.

Mr. Billings looks different
in clothes.
Important.
He's wearing a black suit
and patent leather loafers.
His midnight-blue tie's so shiny,
it looks metallic.

"Hello, Shasten."

"Hi," she squeaks.

He nods at me.

I can't tell if he's displeased,
annoyed, or angry.
I can tell he's agitated, though.
His energy's at a rolling boil,
like hot lava
about to break his calm surface.

"What's your name?"

"W—William, sir."

"*Sir*. Yes, you're the one."

"Excuse me?"

"The one who gave me the massage?"

"Yes, sir."

"Good. I wanted to talk to you both
so there'd be no misunderstanding."

316

He reaches in his back pocket, but
doesn't find whatever he's looking for.

"Shasten's been my body worker
for over a year . . . but you . . ."

He pats his suit pockets,
continuing his search,
and catches my eye.

"I'm sorry, sir, if I—"

> "No, no," Billings interrupts.
> "I'm the one who's sorry."

He keeps fumbling in his jacket pocket.

"If I hurt you,
it wasn't intentional."

> "*Hurt* me?"

His eyes bug out.
He purses his lips.

Shasten winces.

Then Billings bursts out in a
belly-busting laugh.

> "I've never felt better!"

What?

"Ah! Here it is!"
Billings pulls out his wallet.

He hands me two one-hundred-dollar bills.

"I've been very happy
with Shasten's work,
but last night
something special
happened."

He takes my hands, flips them over,
inspecting them as if he expects
to find webbing or suction cups.

"You've got a gift, young man.
Something rare and wonderful.
You didn't *hurt* me.
You *cured* me,
and I wanted to thank you in person."

Billings smiles broadly, then checks his Rolex.

"Gotta jet, but I'll be seeing you again soon."

He walks out of Zillah's office
just as his cell phone rings.

Zillah glares at me.

"If I wasn't a pacifist,
I'd totally kick your ass, William."

"What? Why?"

"You put my business in jeopardy.
You can't just do body work
on clients."

Zillah slams a piece of paper down on her desk.

"Sign this."

I sign the paper,
hoping that
will stop Zillah
from glaring at me.

"You are now an apprentice.
If you complete five hundred hours of training,
you can become certified."

Shasten's shaking her head.

"Mr. Billings was in a car accident
three years ago. The whiplash caused
him so much pain, he started coming in
every few days to get relief."

She looks at me.

"And now he's cured?"

"I just did what you showed me."

"Mr. Billings saw things
while you were working
on him," Zillah says to me.

"Glowing orbs and bits of flame.
He felt extreme heat, chilling cold,
and his bones cracking.
And he loved it. At least
that's what he told me."

I shrug.

"William, if you don't mind,
I'm going to contact some friends
about this. About you."

"About *me*? Why?"

"If you're as gifted
as Mr. Billings says,
my friends will want to meet you."

"Coolness."

I hold up my hundred-dollar bills.

"Ice cream, anyone?"

"That's the least you can do
after stealing my best client."
Shasten laughs.

Inky Shapes

Zillah gives Shasten and me
the rest of the night off.

Shasten's so excited,
she's hopping around
like a little kid.

She grabs my hand
and pulls me up to the solarium.

> "I *knew* it!"

"Knew what?"

> "That you're an *empath*.
> Like me!"

She hugs me.

> "And that's why I can't get a read on you."

"An empath? Are you kidding?
But I don't get a *read* on anyone."

"But you *do*. You read that kid, Patches.
I think if you'll just open your mind,
you'll see you've been reading people
for a long time."

Is she the crazy one now?
I wonder . . .
I *did* hear screams and cries.
I *did* see energy during Shasten's massage.
And I guess I *did* heal Mr. Billings' neck problem.

"Come on, let's meditate,"
Shasten says, lighting incense.

I close my eyes.
I breathe in through my nose,
exhale out my mouth.
I take a deep breath in
and pause.
As soon as I exhale,
I feel myself fall.

Fall into the darkness.

My bones are heavy,
like they're filled with lead.

My breaths are wings,
like they're lifting me.

The space between breaths
is weightless.
Gravity-defying.

But as I linger in this space,
levitating in my mind,
I'm sensing gloom.

Inky shapes flank me,
moving to intercept me.
And now I'm sensing dread.

The inky shapes attack,
flinging themselves at me.
They cling, enclose, and suffocate.

I can't breathe.
I can't move.
I can't see.

"William? William?"

I snap out of my meditation,
gasping and coughing.

"Are you okay?"

"Yeah, I think so."

I shake off the darkness.

"You know,
if I'm an empath,
I'm afraid my future
isn't looking so bright."

"What do you mean?
What did you see?"

"Dark things."

"That's never happened to me,
but it doesn't sound good.
We should stop for tonight."

"Yeah."

I Scream

"So is your invitation still open?"

"Which one?"

"To go out for ice cream."

"Yeah, sure."

"I know a great place.
Oh wait, my aunt has my car.
I'll just text her to pick me up there."

We leave the spa,
head toward the beach.

Shasten leads me to a colorful
trailer near the pier
with a sign that reads
DATE SHAKES,
GELATO,
AND WORLD-FAMOUS
FROZEN BANANAS.

They have
a crazy number of
ice cream flavors,
ranging from
jasmine milk tea
to chunky monkey–
cookie creature.

Then they have
toppings galore,
including candy canes,
butter beans,
and gummy drops.

But this is a first for me.
They scoop your ice cream,
sprinkle it with toppings,
then stuff it all into a warm
glazed doughnut.
They call it
a Creamy Cake.

This isn't Kansas anymore.
I'm pretty sure
I've never ordered anything
this decadent in my entire life.

I order a Creamy Cake
filled with choco bunny–
pudding pie ice cream
and topped with
toffee nuts.

Shasten orders two
Creamy Cakes filled with
jasmine milk tea ice cream
topped with strawberry boba.

"Two?"

    "One for my little brother, is that okay?"

"Sure.
I've got money to spare."

              "My brother's got anger issues
              'cause of Mom being so sick.
              I think this'll cheer him up."

I'm almost done with mine
when Shasten tugs on my arm.

              "My aunt's here.
              You want a ride home?"

"Okay, sure."

I follow her
to a silver station wagon.

We pile in the backseat.
Her aunt's rail thin
with a huge forehead.

The boy in the passenger seat
has his hoodie up
and his ear buds in.
I can only see the tip
of his nose.
I assume it's Shasten's
little brother.

              "This is Aunt Brevis
              and my brother, Darwin."

Aunt Brevis nods to me
via the rearview mirror
and pulls the car
away from the curb.

Shasten taps her brother
on the shoulder.
He pulls out his ear buds.

        "I got a Creamy Cake for you."

He takes it from her
without saying a word.

                "Say thank you
                to William.
                He paid."

Darwin turns around
and pulls his hoodie back,
revealing neon red hair.

Freeze-frame me.

Our eyes lock.
For a split second,
I don't think Darwin recognizes
that I'm the one who broke
his collarbone.
But I'm sorely wrong.

Before I can say anything,
Darwin starts screaming.

Jasmine milk tea ice cream
goes all over the car.

Darwin's screams are so loud
and piercing,
my eyes feel
like they're bleeding.

I claw at the door handle.
I have to get out of here.

Darwin attempts to crawl
over the front seat
to get at me.

"Dar, stop!
Calm down!"

Aunt Brevis gets kicked
in the head.

"Knock it off right now, Dar!"

I get the door open
and leap out.

I skid and slide
across the asphalt,
then crab crawl
to the safety
of the curb.

Banged Up

I limp home.

My Chucks
are ruined.
The toe of my right
one's ripped off.
The left one's
missing the
canvas over the ankle.

I've got road rash
down my left arm,
and a bloody lump
on my forehead.

I come in the back door
and fall onto my cot.

     "William?"

Dad's the last person
I want to see.

"Yes, sir?"

     "William, get your ass out here. Now!"

What have I done?

I follow Dad through the kitchen.

     "Hello, Fl—William."

Coach and the two cops from school
are waiting in the TV room.

"What happened to you, son?"
one of the cops asks.

"Um, I was running
and fell."

"You must be fast."

"He is," Coach says.
"Flash, these officers and I
are here because a teacher's
reported a suspicious
boy hanging around
her preschool.
She managed to get a picture."

The cop shows
Dad a blurry picture
on his phone.
Dad shrugs,
looks over at me.

The cop shows me his phone.

Freeze-frame me.

No one can tell
it's me in that photo,
but Coach was there.
He knows.

What do I say?
How much do I tell them?

How do I explain that I
see and hear this little boy
all the time?
That I know he's being
abused?

Hi, I'm William,
I'm an empath.
I know this kid needs help.

Crazy? Me?

I'm only crazy
if I expect them to
believe me.

I only need to give them
an explanation for what
they already know.

Start my heart.

     "We can't make out the boy,"
     the cop says,
     "but the car can clearly be seen."

     "That's how they found me,"
     Coach says.
     "You're the only one
     I've had in my car recently,
     so here we are."

     "Have you been
     at that preschool?"
     Dad demands.

Hail Mary,
here we go.

"I *have* been by the preschool,
but only twice.
I know this might look bad, but
it's not what you think.
I have a really good reason."

They're waiting.

"I was in class and saw
this little kid outside
all alone.
I wanted to help him,
find out where he belonged."

The cops are studying my every move,
listening to any variation of inflection,
searching for breaks in logic.

I make sure to breathe
in a calm, regular, normal fashion.
I make sure my posture's relaxed.
But inside I'm going apeshit,
racking my brain for an out.

"I followed him to the preschool.
Then I went back to let them know
he'd been out and they should
be watching their kids better."

I shrug.

"I mean, what would
I want with a little boy?"

"You tell us, William.
What would you want
with a little boy?"

This cop's got some nerve.

The smart ass in me wants to say,
"Play Jenga, toss a football, or read Dr. Seuss,"
but all I can say is, "Nothing.
I'm telling you the truth.
There's a little kid out there
who needs help."

"See, Officer?"
Coach sounds relieved.
"I told you he'd have
a good explanation."

One of the cops motions at Coach.

"So this kid's on your team?"

Coach nods.

"Would it be okay if I got a picture
of the player and the coach?"

Are you shitting me?
Really?
How did this turn into a photo op?
I don't want to do this,
but Coach agrees and
puts his arm around me.

And then that's it.
The paparazzi-cops leave.
Unbelievable.

I start back to my room,
but Dad follows me.

> "William, this is *not* cool.
> Any involvement with the police
> can cause a ton of problems for me
> at work."

"Sorry, sir.
I understand."

> "Do you?
> I mean, I could lose my job.
> So you'd better be telling the truth."

"I am. I swear."

> "If the cops show up here again,
> get ready for the military."

The Tree

My phone got smashed when
I jumped out of the car,
so I can't text Shasten.

How is it possible
that of all the people
here, I break the collarbone
of the asshat brother
of the girl I love?

This is a total clusterfuck.

I can't stop thinking about
Patches.
Why does no one but me
care about this kid?

If I can just find him, I can prove
I'm not some disgusting creep,
not like the people hurting him.
I'd prove I'm actually
a pillar of goodness,
a hero.

But where is he?
Shasten's probably right
that *Patches*
isn't even his real name.

I decide to try to link to him
one more time.

I kick off my ripped-up Chucks,
then strip off all of my clothes.
I sit cross-legged
in the middle of my room
on the floor.

The tile's cold on my ass,
but it sort of feels good.

I close my eyes
and breathe . . .

Let myself fall
into the darkness.

I'm floating on black clouds,
searching for light.

Breathe.

My bones are heavy.

Breathe.

I can just make out a road
lined with hedges.

There's a park
with kids' playground
equipment.

It seems familiar
somehow.

I walk past the park,
past the swing set,
past the slide,
past the monkey bars.

Across the road,
a tall gnarled tree
rises up from a yard,
shading a green house
with white trim.

A white sedan
with gold wheels
is parked in the driveway.

There's arguing.
A woman's voice.
And a man's.

A slim man with slicked-back hair
and a thin mustache
comes out of the house.

He's searching for me.

I don't like him.

He's going to take me away.
He's going to hurt me.

I scramble up into the tree.
Climb higher
and higher.

I climb past a bird's nest,
past a knot in the trunk,
past a crook with a mangled branch.

I climb up high
into the thin branches.

The breeze pushes me.
I sway with the tree.

Frantically, I grab
at the thin branches,
try to steady myself.

A branch breaks,

        and

      I

           fall.

Reset

I snap alert.

The sun's coming up.

It seems like I've been sitting here
for just a few minutes,
but I've been here all night.

I'm refreshed,
rejuvenated, and
renewed.

Strange.
The road rash on my left arm
looks a lot less severe,
almost healed.

The lump on my forehead's
almost gone.

This is so fucking strange.

I put on clean clothes,
slip on my hiking boots.
Something's driving me
to get going.
I'm itchy.
I need to get out of the house.

I've got to walk.
Gotta clear my mind
so I can think.

'Napped

I'm out the back door
and into the alley.

I don't know where I'm going,
but I don't think school's
on my schedule today.

The park I saw
through Patches' eyes—
I've seen it before.
I know it's somewhere ahead of me,
like a ghost GPS
whispering a turn by turn
in my ears.

I stop cold in my tracks.

The bushy brown dog's
standing in the middle of the alley.
His ears are twitching, rotating
like he's listening
for something specific.
His pale blue eyes watch me
with intensity.
The fur on his neck
and shoulders rises.

Suddenly he lunges toward me.
He's incredibly fast.
Before I can react,
he sweeps past me.

I snap around.
He turns a corner,
his dust cloud in the air.

Should I follow him?

Too late.

Everything goes black.

A nylon bag's jerked down over my head.
It smells like rubber and sweat.
Strong hands are grabbing my arms.

"What the—?"

I'm knocked over.

Muffled whispers.
Shoes shuffling on asphalt.

Duct tape's wrapped around
my wrists and ankles.

I'm dragged a few feet,
then lifted
into the trunk of a car
and then we're driving.

What the hell's just happened?

Haze

The trunk opens.

"Who the fuck are you?"

> "Chill, bro.
> What were you doing
> outside so early?
> The walk of shame?"

They free my feet
and yank me out.

I'm pushed into a cold room.
Sounds echo off hard surfaces.

Someone cuts the duct tape off.
But they leave the hood on.

I'm not alone.
There are whimpers
and movement
all around me.

> "Air raid!"

I'm tackled hard to the floor
by two guys.

It smells like sweat and bleach.

Other boys groan.
Some kid next to me
squeals in pain.

"Ladies, if you make it
through this,
you'll officially be part
of the brotherhood."

Needlemier.
I'd know his voice anywhere.
This must be some sort of team hazing,
how he'll get back at me.

The inky black things
are suddenly closing in on me,
smothering my aura,
my energy, and my light.

"Unhood them."

Someone yanks off my hood.

I blink hard.

We're in the locker room.
A single overhead light
creates a cone of illumination
around us.

I count five new team members
in the middle
of the locker room.

Jim's to my far left.

Two sophomores
whose names I don't know
are to his right.

Teddy the freshman's
next to me,
looking like he's gonna cry.

We're surrounded
by a dozen wolves.
I recognize the shoes and body types.
Needlemier and his meatheads
are all wearing plastic wolf masks
and wielding wooden paddles.

"Welcome to the brotherhood
of the wolves."

Needlemier's words
set them all howling.
The coarse, eerie sounds echo
off the lockers and the tile.

"Now, brothers!"

The light goes out.

I'm hit in the stomach,
then shoved to the floor.

Bodies on top of me.

I'm pulled, tugged, and pushed
over on my knees and elbows.

I try to get free, but there are
too many of them
holding me down.

"What the fuck are you doing?!"

"Relax, man.
It ain't nothing."

Swats,
thumps,
cries.

A hard swat.
Teddy screams.

Swat!
A paddle finds my left butt cheek.
Son of a bitch, that hurts!
I flinch, but keep quiet.
Won't give them the satisfaction.

The swatting stops.
Teddy's crying for real now.

"Again. This time bare ass."

Hands grab at my ankles.
I'm yanked flat onto my stomach.
Fingers fumble with my jeans.

"Stop!" someone yells.

My jeans and boxers are yanked down.

I'm wrestled back onto my knees.

The swats start again.
The smacks and cries are louder.

Teddy whines.

> "Hey, you fuckwads,
> he's had enough."

I brace for another swat.

> "Hold up! This one's mine."

Needlemier looms over me.
Hands and arms
change position
but don't loosen
their grip.

They're making way
for their leader.

> "You get something special,
> you goddamn queer."

Fuck you,
Needlemier.

I brace for impact,
but nothing happens.

Then
I feel his fat fingers
crawling up my butt crack.

"I've been wanting to do this
for a long time.
Where's that chocolate starfish?"

His fingers push and pull.

"Get your hands out of my ass!"

That freezes the guys holding me,
but not Needlemier.

His finger jerks
and jams
against my anus.

Goddamn it!
I squeeze my butt cheeks tight.

He shoves his finger up my ass
as far as it can go.

I roar.
I pull, tug, and kick.

"Get your finger
out of my asshole,
Needlemier!
You fucking pervert!"

　　　　"What are you doing, man?
　　　　I didn't sign on for this."

"Shut the hell up!
William likes it.
I'm just giving him
what he asked for."

The hands holding me loosen
for a second.
And that's just enough time.
I grab a mouthful of the wrist
in front of me and bite down. Hard.

"Wooaaaaah!"

I slam the back of my head
into the chin of whoever's holding
my right shoulder.

"Hold the perv down!
Keep holdin' him!"

I orient on Needlemier's screams
and rush him.
"Fuck you, Needlemier!"

He punches me in the face
and shoulder, but I dive in close.
I wrap my arms around his chest
and lift him off the floor.
Blind rage fuels my legs and I drive him
full-force back into the lockers.

His head smashes into the metal door.

There's shouting and chaos.
The lights come on.

Pummeling Needlemier's face
brings him into submission.
But I'm not seeking a settlement.
Not now.
I'm seeking retribution.

I grab Needlemier's head,
push my thumbs into his eyes.
I squeeze hard, but can't pop the cantaloupe,
so I slam it into the locker door.

Slam!

Slam!

Slam!

There's dents in the gray steel.
Gray that's turning red
from the blood.

> "You're gonna kill 'im,
> you crazy son of a bitch!"

I'm grabbed by many hands
and pulled off that motherfucker.

"Leave me alone!"
I'm growling,
panting.

Needlemier isn't moving.

349

No "Me"

No one dares look at me.

Teddy's crying.

I jerk up my jeans.

The wolf masks are scattered
across the locker room.
Most of the guys are making a quick exit.

> "That fucker crossed the line,"
> Jim mutters.

> "I'm calling an ambulance!"
> Bender says, his hand shaking
> as he tries to dial 9-1-1.

> "Fuck him. I'm calling the cops!"
> Teddy says.

That's my cue to beat it.

I guess there's no "me"
in team.

Origins

I'm running.
I don't know where I'm going.
I'm just running.

Somehow I'm back in the alley,
where those assholes kidnapped me.

I stand there for what seems
like hours.

The dog.
I should've followed that dog
when he ran past me.
It's like he knew
something bad
was about to happen.

And just as I'm thinking this,
the blue-eyed dog's
there in the alley.

He's shaking himself
like he's just come out of
the ocean,
but he doesn't look wet.

The dog barks at me.
Is he saying,
"I told you so"?

He turns, then lopes off.

I follow him.
I'm not letting him out of my sight.

He leads me through back alleys
and down deserted streets.

He keeps just ahead of me;
just in sight but not too close.

We turn down a road.
I get a deep sense of *déjà vu.*
I've been here before.

A park comes into view
to the right.

It looks old.
Overgrown.

There's a stagnant pond
with a couple of ducks
swimming in it.

The dog trots farther ahead of me.

I jog to keep up,
but he's moving faster.

As I come to a playground,
I lose sight of him.

There's an old rusty swing set,
paint bubbled and cracked,
one of the seats missing.

Graffiti covers the slide,
the rungs of the ladder broken
or gone.

Rusty monkey bars
are shattered in three places.

"Where are you, boy?"

Damn!
He's really gone again.
As I'm looking around
for the dog,
I see a tall gnarled tree
rising out
of a yard across the road.

The tree's shading
a green house
with white trim.

The thin branches
at the top of the tree
sway in the breeze.

The leaves sing
and rattle.

In a kind of trance,
I cross the road
to the yard.

Standing under
the tree,
I look over at the house:

every plant,
every brick,
every detail
is the same
as what I saw in my mind last night.
The same as what I saw
through Patches' eyes.

I search the branches above me.
There's the bird's nest
and the knot hole
and the crook with the mangled branch.

A familiar giggle
comes from behind me.

I whip around.

"Patches?!"

Little shoes step inside the house
and the front door slams.

I rush to the front porch
and look in the windows,
but I can't see inside.

I check the door.
It's unlocked.

The furniture's old,
pretty threadbare,
but still functional,
like the coffee table
with lion's claw feet.

Persian rugs cover all the dark
hardwood floors.

Little feet running,
the noise kind of muffled
on the rugs.

"Patches?"

> "I hide and you seek.
> Look behind you, see today.
> Bleeding from your eyes."

I follow his voice to a bedroom.

It's an old woman's room judging
by the furniture and the smell:
pine and mothballs.

"Patches?"

> "You left me behind.
> I could not jump high enough.
> They cannot reach me."

His voice is coming from under the bed.

I climb onto the mattress.
A pair of pale blue eyes peek
up at me between the headboard
and the mattress.

"Is this your house?"

       "Dirty little boy.
       The woman sucked my pee-pee.
       Don't you remember?"

"How can I remember
what happened to *you*?"

I glance at a small framed photo
resting in the headboard shelf.

A woman's holding a kid
on her lap.
In front of them
a dog's playing
with a ball.

A bushy brown dog.

I pick up the photo.

It's the same dog
that's led me here.
Only he doesn't have pale blue eyes.

What the hell?

I look down between the mattress
and the headboard.

Patches is gone.

"Patches?"

I look around the room.
Where is he?

How could he just vanish?

Then I see a photo album
on the dresser.

The cover has a photo of
a car on it.
A white sedan with gold wheels.

I rifle through the pages.

There!
There's a picture of the
little boy I know
as Patches.

He's wearing
the same red flannel shirt,
the same jeans, and
the same sneakers.

The caption below
the photo says
William, age 4.

Patches

"Patches, come!"

The bushy brown dog
hops into the backseat
of the white sedan.

His tail's wagging so fast,
he can barely stand.

"Where are we going?"

     "Not far."

She starts the car,
and we back out the driveway.

The morning's cloudy
and cold.

The seagulls at the beach seem angry.
They're crying, diving,
and screaming at each other.

We drive for almost an hour.

We finally stop at
the end of a long dirt road.

     "Patches probably has to pee.
     Why don't you take him
     for a walk, okay?"

"Okay."

I open the back door
and we pile out,
my dog and I,
one ball
of nervous energy.

I look around,
but it's all concrete.

> "There's grass
> on the other side."

I look to where she's pointing.

On the other side of
a chain-link fence
is lots of green, green grass.

I pick up Patches.
I have to climb
up the chain-link fence
a couple of feet,
but I'm able to get him
over.

I plop over the other side
with him.

Patches barks,
running and hopping
in circles around me.

"Come on, boy!
Tag, you're it!"
We race across the grass.

The car engine starts up.

It's too soon.
I don't want to leave yet.
Patches is having too much fun.

     "William, we have to go."

Patches chases me
as I run back to the fence.

     "Leave him."

"What?"

     "Leave him."

"But I can't."

     "Leave the dog. Now."

She starts driving slowly away.

"I can't.
Don't make me."

She drives farther down the road.

"I'll come back, boy.
I promise."

I hug my dog around his neck.
I kiss the two blond patches
on his dark brown fur.

She guns the engine,
honks the horn.

"Bye, boy."
I clamber back over the fence.

Patches yelps and
starts to jump at the fence.

The car rolls away faster.

"Stop!
Wait for me!"

She does.
I get into the backseat.
She drives us away before
I can even get the door closed.

I turn in my seat and
wave through the back window
as my bushy brown dog frantically
throws himself at the chain-link fence.

"Patches.
Patches.
Patches . . ."

Tidal Wave

I fling the photo album
on the green chair
and stumble off the bed.

I can't find solid footing.
The floor oozes and swells
like the ocean floor
ravaged by
a tidal wave.

I can't catch my breath.
I'm caught halfway
between sobbing and vomiting.

I know this place.

I know this place
because I lived here once.

Remembering

Everywhere

I

look,

the

nightmares

of

my

past

come

to

life.

Yellow Sofa

I'm sitting on
the new neon-yellow sofa
playing with a truck.

A woman leads a pasty-faced man into the room.

> "William, this is Alistair.
> He's your new friend."

> "Hello, William."

I ignore the man,
continue to play with my truck.
"Vrooom! Vrooom!"

> "I'll leave you two alone."

When the woman leaves,
the man, Alistair, moves next to me.
He smiles down at me.
He has a gold front tooth.

He tugs at my shoes
and pulls them off.

He takes my truck away,
throws it on the floor.

"Don't!"
I begin to struggle,
but his hands are really strong,
and he twists my arms.

He flips me over onto my tummy.
Clumsy fingers pull at my pants.

"Stop it."

"Shhhhh.
We're just playing a game.
Shhhhh."

He covers my mouth.
His hand smells of garlic and fish.
I want to throw up.

He leans over me,
the hairs on his chin digging into my cheek.
The air on my bottom is cold.
I want my blankie.

He pulls me onto my knees.
I sink a little into the yellow sofa cushion.
Something warm and wet
slides down my bottom.
He's spit on me.

PAIN!
He's got his finger in my bottom.

I scream into his stinky hand,
but he just keeps jabbing me
with his finger.

He pulls his finger out.
Is it over?
What did I do
to make him so angry?
I should've stopped
playing with my truck.

He shifts his body over me.
His weight presses me down
into the yellow sofa.

PAIN!
Something big's pushing
inside me.
It's too big.
I'm going to rip.

He grunts.
The hairs on his chin
scrape my cheek like
a cheese grater.

Then he's gone.

Tears blur my vision.
I can't breathe.

I will not play with my truck.
I will not play with my truck.
I will not play with my truck.

I hate that truck.

I lie on my tummy,
shivering,
on the yellow sofa.

"How was my little William, Alistair?"

"Consider your rent covered."

Persian Rug

The woman kneels in front of me
and pulls down my pants.

> "I need to teach you something.
> So pay attention."

She runs her hands down
my shoulders.
She caresses my arms,
my chest,
my waist.

She lifts my pee-pee
between her thumb
and forefinger.

> "You are a dirty little boy.
> I'm going to have to clean this."

She cups my pee-pee,
like she's weighing it.
She tickles my bottom
with her pink fingernails.

> "It's so sweet.
> I like it when it's soft."

I want to tell her to stop it,
but then she lowers her head
and puts my pee-pee
in her mouth.

I gasp.

It's warm,
and it's soft.

I don't like it,
but I like her.

Why is she doing this?

She's bobbing her head
back and forth.

What's happening to me?
My body shudders.
I feel sorta sick.

My pee-pee
flops out of her mouth,
and she sits up.

> "Now, can you remember
> what I just taught you?"

I nod.

> "Good.
> Because you'll have to do that
> to someone else."

Lion's Claw Foot Table

I'm naked,
standing in the middle of the
living room.

Eight chairs are filled
with people.

Everyone's looking at me.

Some people are smiling at me.
Some people are winking at me.

> "Bidding is open,"
> the woman says.

People are putting money
on the coffee table
with the lion's claw feet
in front of them.

The woman makes me
spin
around slowly.

Money piles higher.

> "Now do what I showed you."

I want to please her,
to show her I remember
what she taught me.
I pull on my pee-pee.

Some people laugh.
Some people clap their hands.

One man reaches out and
touches my leg,
then adds more money
to the pile
on the table.

"We have a winner."

The woman takes my hand,
leads me to the man.

"Now do what I taught you."

The man unzips his pants.

Recognizing

My

memories

are

like

a

riptide

pulling

me

deeper

into

the

dark

sea.

The Woman

I finally steady myself,
glance around the room.

When did I live here?
How could I live these things?
Who is that woman?

I pick up the photo album.
Some pictures have come unglued
from the pages,
including some photos
of a wedding.

The woman
of my nightmares
is the bride
in these photos.

She's all by herself
in her white gown.

Except in one photo.

Her veil's pulled back
and she's looking into the eyes
of the groom.

He's slim with slicked-back hair
and a thin mustache.

It hits me
before I even read
the wedding invitation
taped to the back of the photo.

The rail-thin groom
in the photo
is my father.

And that woman,
that woman who used me
as barter,
that woman who molested me,
that woman who fed me
to sexual predators,
is
my
mother.

Imploding

My world is imploding.

The shiny metropolis
I once called my life
has been built upon
the shifting sands of lies.

The dunes, dikes, and dams
I've built have burst.
The raging sea
has flooded
my lands.

There will be no
harvest of crops.
Nothing grows
here now.

My memories
latch onto my lungs,
liver,
and kidneys
like Gramps' cancer.

Like black inky monsters,
they dig their claws in,
then squeeze,
extract,
crush.

My heart bleeds
the atramentous,
putrid sludge
of sorrow.

I have no right
to judge others.
Not
Needlemier,
Bender,
the Edlebachers,
or
Darwin.

I have no right
to ask for love.

I have no right to live.

Breathe

Live or die?
That's the question I ask
with every breath.
Continue to live,
or stop altogether?

Breathe

A breath only allows you to exist.
You must engage.
Venture forth.
Tangle yourself with others to have a life.
But life needs a purpose or what's the point?

Breathe

The point . . .

The point stares back at me.
Silver with gray lines where the machining sharpened it.
Nine inches of hardened steel.
A comfortable wood handle.
Only $4.99 at Bed Bath and Beyond.

Breathe

Beyond . . .

Beyond the optic nerve.
Cornea, iris, viscous body, retina.
If I get the ice pick beyond my eye,
I could reach the frontal lobe.
Where the memories live.
But I'll have to dig around
once the ice pick gets into my brain.
Swirl, dig, search, find
hideous memories hiding in their temple.

Breathe

Temple . . .

My temple.
The pterion bone is the thinnest spot
in our skulls, just behind our eyes
and in front of our ears.
I could go in sideways,
shove the ice pick straight in, then up.
Swirl, dig, search, erase.
But I might puncture the middle meningeal artery.
Does that matter? Not today.

Breathe

Today . . .

Today. Right now.
This very instant.
Who am I?

At any moment in time, we are the sum
of our experiences.
The average of our highs and lows
in the life we have played out.
The characters we have portrayed.
The truths we have embellished.
The lies we have told.
The facts we have omitted.
The life I once knew is all lies.

Breathe

Lies . . .

There are so many
different ways to tell one.
Willful false testimony,
slander,
deception,
or omission.
The network of falsehoods,
half-truths,
and distortions
are impossible to balance.

Breathe

Balance . . .

Karma is in balance.
It keeps account
of debits
and credits.
I thought I had
a bright future,
but only because
I discounted
my history.

Breathe

History . . .

My history was
forced on me.
I did not ask for it.
But I can never
be free from it.
It is an equal part
of my recipe.

Live or die?
Live or die?
Live . . . die.

Why can't I do both?

Pretty Sure

The afternoon sun
sizzles through
the windows.

I rifle through
the kitchen drawers.

Dull knives,
nothing menacing,
except the ice pick.

I slip it
into my pocket,
just in case.

I'm pretty sure
this isn't the path
I should take.

Not now.
Now that I've linked
all the events
in my timeline
together.

I'm pretty sure
I lived with my
so-called
mother
until I was six.

Pretty sure G'ma and Gramps
didn't know this
was happening to me.
That I was a sex toy.

Pretty sure Dad
was too busy
with Camelot
to remember me.

Pretty sure
there's no football
in my future.

Pretty sure the cops
are looking
for Needlemier's killer.

Pretty sure Shasten
will never talk to me
again.

Pretty sure I'm
headed to jail.

Pretty sure
I won't survive in there.

Pretty sure
my mother hasn't changed.

Pretty sure
she still lives here.

So I'm pretty sure
I'll be back.

OOH-RAH!

The marine layer
is blowing in.

I think I can do
what I need to do
and not be seen.

I locate the house
where I saw Patches
the very first time.

The woman's Volvo
isn't in the driveway.

I crouch by the back door
and shove my arm
through the doggie door.

With a little stretch,
I undo the latch
and I'm in.

I pull on the cabinet doors.
They're locked.
Protecting people
from people like me.

No matter.
I kick the door
until the wood
splinters.
I take the .45
semi-automatic.

It only holds seven bullets
in the magazine
versus fourteen in the 9mm,
but these big bullets
will put a man down
with one shot.

I like the 308 Winchester rifle.
It looks like the most accurate,
but long-distance shooting's
not in my plan.

No.
Today calls for
up close and personal,
maximum damage
with minimum effort.

The woman's husband
must be a cop,
because there's a perfect
12-gauge tactical shotgun
in the collection.

I exit the way I came in,
but with a much heavier
load.

As I reach the end of the driveway,
headlights wash across me.

I break into a run as
the Volvo
drives past me.

Pep Rally

I rush through the alleys
and side streets.
I keep to the shadows.

Don't need any eyes on me.

I keep searching for the blue-eyed dog,
even though I know he's not real.

I wish he were
trotting ahead of me,
guiding me.

The off-shore breeze
blows in a heavy wet fog,
a thick-like-whipped-cream fog.

I'm pretty sure
my school's on
this street.
Pretty sure.

I've been walking
for twenty minutes,
but there's no
line of mommy-cars,
and no Mini Mart on the corner.

A weird sound's
reverberating around me:
a rhythmic pounding,
deep bass and tribal.

A glow emerges from the fog.

It's a bonfire.

I walk across the parking lot
toward the fire.

Brinlee's leading her cheerleaders
in kicks and hops,
cheers, and dance routines
to the drumbeat.

It's a pep rally
in the parking lot
at my school.

I stand under a tree,
hidden by the fog.

I watch everyone
like a lion
watches gazelles:
sizing them up,
looking for weakness,
gauging distance.

I cycle the slide
of the .45 to load
the first round,
and cock the hammer back.

It's heavy.
Not because it's made of steel.
It's heavy because it has the power
over life and death.

Someone's coming out of the fog.
Coming toward me.

I slowly lift the pistol.

"I thought I might find you here."

I look at Ollie.
Then see I'm standing
under our tree.
Ollie's and mine.

"Why are they having a pep rally?
Don't they know Needlemier's dead?"

"What?
Needlemier isn't *dead*.
You gave him one nasty
cracked skull, but he's not dead.
Geez, you thought you killed him?"

"Too bad."

"Where have you been?
They're searching for you
everywhere, you know."

"At my mother's house."

"The school counselor says you have
a history of violence. That you
moved here after assaulting two
brothers."

"You talked to her?"

"She was on the news."

"Did she also say
those brothers
were raping a friend
of mine?
A fourteen-year-old girl."

"No. She didn't say that.
That's horrible."
He stomps his foot.
"Why is it that the innocent always
get hurt? Why do the rapists
and bullies go unpunished?"

"That's a good question,
Ollie. You ask very
good questions."

I suddenly realize I've been
pointing the gun
at Ollie all this time.

"Shit. Sorry, Ollie."

I lower the gun.

"I know you wouldn't
shoot a friend.
I know you wouldn't
shoot an innocent person.
That's not in your makeup."

"I don't know, Ollie.
I've got some bad
ideas in my head.
Really bad."

Sirens.
Red and blue lights flash in the fog.
The police are coming.

"Sorry, William.
I called them a little while ago,
when I saw you here.
You don't have to do this.
Teddy and Bender said
Needlemier crossed the line.
Just put down the gun."

"Ollie, I've changed my answer."

"To what?"

"My biggest triumph . . .
is friending you."

Black Helmet

Ollie's right.

It's not in my makeup
to shoot an innocent person.
And yet here I am,
plotting to shoot up
the pep rally.

Ollie's words keep
ringing in my head.

> "Why is it that the innocent always
> get hurt? Why do the rapists
> and bullies go unpunished?"

My logic's been flawed,
my path misdirected,
and my rage misspent.

Suicide by cop is
a very entertaining thought.
All I need to do is just start shooting,
but these people don't deserve that.
No one at the rally deserves that.

I want to emerge
from that long dark tunnel
wearing a black helmet.

I want to hear people
whisper, "It's Flash, it's Flash,"
as I pass by.

I want Shasten
to wear my 00 jersey.

But I want acceptance
and approval,
not fear.

After my fight with
the Edlebachers,
Gramps said,
"There's a ton of bad,
scary,
filthy
crap in the world,
and it doesn't end
at your doorstep.
It flows into the cracks
in the foundation
of your most sacred places.
It finds a way to flood, to rise,
and to fill.
You might not see it,
not right away,
but you'll smell it.

You did a good thing
saving that girl,
but you let them pull
you down into the filth.
Now, you're gonna have to work
really hard to get your life back."

I think I understand his message.
Darwin pulled me down.
Needlemier pulled me down.
My mother and Alistair pulled me down.

I want my life back.

The Fog

A few quick steps
and I'm alone
in the fog.

The cops will be busy
looking for me
at the rally.

I keep to the shadows,
avoid the light,
especially any flashing
red or blue.

I quiet my thoughts
and focus my mind.

I try to become
like the fog.

It's easy
because
I am nothing.

Green Chair

The window's
open like I left it.
I listen to the silence
for a moment,
then climb inside.

Back in the bedroom,
I sit in the green chair
that faces the bed.

The green chair that used
to always have clothes
strewn across it.

At least that's how
I remember it.
I guess that's why

it's the only piece
of furniture
I'm comfortable
sitting on.

Because it's the only
piece of furniture
in the entire house.
where I didn't
get fucked.

The green house with white trim
was my grandmother's house.
My mother moved us here after Dad left.

My mother's mother
never liked me.
In fact, she hated me.

She once told me
she wished I was dead.
I was three or four
at the time.

I don't know why
she hated me so much.
Maybe she blamed me
for being dirty.

As much as she
hated me,
my mother
loved me.

My mother
thought I was
beautiful.
She thought I was
sent from heaven.

I had no idea
she thought I was
her meal ticket.

I had no idea
she thought I was
disposable.

Light
from a car's headlights
bounces across the walls.
Old brakes squeal.
Car doors open,
then thump closed.

I sit in the green chair
and I wait
with the shotgun
across my lap
and the .45
in my pocket.

The back door opens.

Lights come on
in the hallway.

Muffled conversation.

Footsteps.

Someone steps into
the bedroom
and switches on the light.

"Hello, Marnie."

          "What the hell?"

My mother stares at me.
She's struggling
with the recognition.

Maybe she's known lots of boys by now.
Or maybe it's the eleven-year
absence from my life
that's making her pause.

She's no longer
the lithe young woman
in the photos.

She's no longer
the physical threat
of a molester.

She's no longer
the seller to the
highest bidder.

She's still
the woman
of my nightmares,
but changed.

She's doughy.
Fuller around her hips
and breasts.

Wrinkles have ravaged
her face,
her blue eyes.

Her neck's loose,
turkey-like.

Her hair's still dark,
but with streaks
of gray framing her face.
Frankenstein's Bride.

"William."

"How rude of me."
I stand up.

She gasps,
seeing the shotgun.

"What, no hugs?"

"What . . . what are you
doing here?"

"I live here now."

She looks confused.
"Oh, wait.
Did you mean here
as in California, or
here as in
your house?"

She shrugs.

"Gramps died.
G'ma's getting older.
I moved here
to live with Dad."

"Marnie? You talkin' to someone?"

A man emerges from the hallway.

"What the hell is this?
Who the fuck are you?"

"It's William.
Do you remember him, Alistair?
This is William.
My son."

Breath to Breath

"Alistair?
Are you shitting me?
Not the same Alistair
who you . . .
from years ago?"

The pasty-faced prick
doesn't answer.
He just shakes his head,
keeping his eyes on the shotgun.

"Goddamn, kid,"
he says with nervous laughter
that reveals his gold tooth.
"What the hell you doin'
with that gun?"

"The years
haven't been kind
to you, Alistair."

"What do you want, William?
After all this time . . .
what do you want?"

"Well, Marnie,
I'd been hoping
for a reunion
with you.
With Alistair here,
it makes tonight even
more special.

You see,
I'd forgotten
all the shit
you did to me
as a kid
when I lived here.

Seems I'd
repressed
all my memories
of my time here.
All of them."

Alistair sighs.
Is he relieved?

I smile.
Not a smile
that says, "I'm happy to see you."
It's the smile a coyote
gives to a bird
on the ground
with a broken wing.

"But I remember now.
All of it.
And I'm considering
blasting you to hell.
Both of you."

I wiggle the shotgun
toward the living room.

"Move!"

I back them up
into the living room.

"Sit!"

They sit down on the yellow couch.
I settle on the lion's claw foot table
across from them.

"This will do."

I lift the shotgun,
click off the safety.

> "Wait.
> William.
> Things have changed.
> *I've* changed."

Is she kidding?

> "Just listen to your mother."

Alistair raises his hands in the air,
pleading.
What a pussy.

Breathe

Live or die.
Live or die.
Live or die . . .

Breathe

"Okay.
I guess
the condemned
deserve to speak
one last time.
What do you want to say,
Mother?"

 "Things were bad
 back then.
 You don't remember
 because you were
 just a little kid.

 Your dad was a drunk.
 He beat me all the time.
 I finally had enough.
 When he left . . .
 when he abandoned us,
 well, I had no job.
 No way to support us."

Breathe

Live or die.
Live or die.
Live or die . . .

Breathe

"So you
traded me
for rent?"

"It was wrong," Alistair says.
"We know that.
We did what we had to do."

"Shut the hell up, asshole."
I aim the shotgun
at him ever so slightly.

I think I'll kill him first.

"But we've changed, William.
We've learned from our
mistakes."

"*Mistakes*, Marnie?
Is that what you think
selling me,
hurting me,
raping me
were? *Mistakes*?"

Breathe

Live or die.
Live or die.
Live or die . . .

Breathe

"Nothing to say?
And why should
it make a difference
to me that you think
you've *changed*?"

"Because we're doing good now.
Repenting for our past sins."

I can't help laughing
at this woman's blindness.

She points at her purse
on the table next to me.

"May I?"

I nod.

She grabs the purse,
struggles to pull
something out.

Alistair seems tense.
And not just because
I have a shotgun aimed
at him.

He's jumpy, acting like there's
a bomb
under the table
set to go off
in thirty seconds.

Marnie thrusts
a crumpled pamphlet at me.

SAINT ALPHONSUS' CHILDREN'S FOUNDATION
Don't abandon your children.
Let us find them a home.

It describes places
where young teens
or homeless mothers
can leave their kids.

"So what?
You've found God
and now you think you're
some angel of mercy
helping *children*?"

        "We help abandoned kids
        find homes, William," she says.
        Whether it's foster care,
        or temporary shelter
        with Child Services.
        Parents can leave
        their kids with us
        and not fear persecution."

"You shouldn't be
anywhere *near* children!
It's you who should
fear prosecution!"

Is that sirens?

I glance out the window,
but don't see
any activity on the street.

        "We're saving kids
        from being abused . . .
        like you were."

"What did I tell you, asshole?
Shut the hell up."

Breathe

Live or die.
Live or die.
Live or die . . .

Breathe

      "We're doing good work now,
      William. You have
      to believe me, son."

"You've mistaken me
for someone else.
I'm not your son.
I'm your executioner. "

All of a sudden
I feel another set of eyes
on me.

The bushy brown dog's
standing by the yellow sofa.

Behind the Door

The dog stretches his legs,
starts trotting down the hall,
looks back at me.

"Get up. Move!"

> "William?
> What are you doing?
> Where are we going?"

I force them ahead of me
down the hall.

The dog's
sniffing at a door
at the back of the house.

> "There's nothing in there!"

Alistair's way too jumpy.

"What're you hiding?"

The dog's vanished.

Then I hear a muffled scream.

"Who the hell's in there?"

The door's locked.
I kick it a few times,
but it's a metal door.

> "William, that's just a storage room!"

I aim the shotgun
at the knob
and fire.

The door blows inward.

"No!"

A man
in a black latex bodysuit's
standing over
a little boy
about five years old.

"What the fuck?!"

The boy's naked,
crying and hunched over
the back of a chair.
His arms and legs are
tied down
with plastic wrap.

Another child,
a little girl, is tied up
to a table.

"It's not what you think!"
Marnie's screaming.
"It's not what it looks like!"

Sirens are wailing clearly now.
Someone's pounding
on the front door.

I pump another shell
into the chamber of the shotgun
and aim it at
the latex perv.

As I pull the trigger,
Alistair knocks me sideways.
My shot misses.

"Shit!"

Alistair wrestles me
to the floor.
He gets a good grip
on the shotgun.

He's strong for
an old fuck.

Latex perv
comes at me
with a knife.

Do I keep
the shotgun
or lose
my life?

I choose my life.

The perv swings the knife
down at my chest.

I let go of the shotgun
and roll out of room.

I come up with the .45 in my hands.

Breathe,
aim,
fire twice,
just like Gramps taught me.

The perv's chest explodes,
double tap.

Alistair fires the shotgun at me.
The shot misses by inches but
drives me backward a step.

"Drop the gun!"

We all turn.
Cops are
in the hallway,
guns drawn and pointed
at me.

Freeze-frame me.

What the cops see
is a crazed kid
with a history of violence,
on a shooting spree,
aiming a pistol
he stole from his neighbor.

What the cops don't see
is a fucked-up mother
with a history of abuse,
selling her kids
to the highest bidder.

What the cops don't see
is her pervert husband
pumping another shell into
a shotgun and
leveling the barrel at me.

Breathe

Live or die.
Live or die.
Live or die . . .

Exhale . . .

I squeeze the trigger
straight back
on the downbeat.

Gunshots fill my ears.

Screams.

Hot
wetness
on my
stomach.

I look down
and see
two bullet holes
in my stomach.

Blood,
bright red,
is staining
my T-shirt.
My blood.

I sink to the floor.

Alistair's already down.
He's coughing blood,
once, twice,
then his eyes glaze over.

Marnie's
standing between
me and the cops.
Her arms are raised,
but she's still denying
she's done
anything
wrong.

I glance into the room
past Alistair,
past Latex perv,
to the little boy
still tied to the chair.

I smile at him,
try to nod.

His face softens
from fright
to relief.

The boy
looks straight
into my eyes
and smiles.

My world goes black.

Live or Die

It's peaceful here.
Like sleeping in on a cold morning
without any school.

There's nothing to see,
nothing to feel,
nothing to hear,
nothing to taste.

But then I hear something.
It's far away
but coming closer.

A ringing in my ears.
Or maybe
it's metal
grinding
on metal.

No. Wait.

It's an alarm, high-pitched and solid.

     "Clear!"
     A man's voice yells.

A shock.
The alarm continues.

     "Clear!"

Shock.
The alarm stops,
then starts again.

It's peaceful here.
But I can't feel anything.
There are no ties,
no supports,
no connections.

The alarm stops,
replaced by
rhythmic
beeping.

> "Breathe!
> Breathe!
> Breathe, you son of a bitch!"

Breathing.
I don't love it
or hate it.
It does not
give me pleasure,
and yet I find it uncomfortable
when it's gone.
I don't remember
my last breath,
or the ones before that.
They were unremarkable.

Breathing only happens
here and now.
But breathing
is my decision.

And I decide to
breathe.

Bio-illogical

My life is a series of snapshots.

Awake,
asleep without dreams,
awake.

Time and consciousness
leap forward.

Sometimes I can talk a little,
other times I can only
observe.

I blink and hours pass.
I blink and the doctor's asking me
if my pain is between one and ten.
I blink and a nurse is wiping my ass.
I blink and I'm half sitting up
in a hospital bed.

       "William?
       Can you hear me?"

I try to say yes,
but there's a tube
in my throat.

I choke.

A nurse rushes to my side.
There's a lot of movement.

I blink and Dad's standing over me.

"Hey, William."

I try to answer,
but my voice
doesn't want to cooperate.

"Your mother.
That Alistair guy.
I blame him."

I blame Alistair for many things,
but it didn't start with him.
Marnie was more than just a passenger.
She put fuel in the tank,
navigated,
and held the steering wheel.

Dad has no idea what happened.
No fucking idea.

"She did some bad things,
but she loves you."

What a fucking idiot.
I try to speak, but all I do is roar.

"Having some pain?"

Loves me?
She traded me for rent.
Stole my innocence
and sold it to pay for a used car.

"Should I call a nurse?"

My voice finally engages.

"Dad, you don't know—"

    "I don't know why you had to
    save those kids on your own."

"Dad, stop.
Listen."

    "You should've called the cops."

"Listen to me."

    "How did you even know
    they were doing that to kids?"

"Because . . . they did it to me."

    "What? What did you say?"

"Dad, before she taught me to read,
she taught me how to give a blow job."

    "What? What are you saying?"

"She traded me.
I was barter."

Dad pales,
grips the bedrail.

"Why didn't I know?
Why didn't I know?"

"Because you were playing horses
with your precious new family.
You left me with that sick bitch.
She doesn't *love* me.
She doesn't know what love means."

"Oh my God. Oh my God.
I'm so sorry. So sorry.
I didn't know.
I'm not defending her—
not at all—
but you should know
she stepped between you
and the cops, William.
She took a bullet for you."

"That's the least she could do.
I'm glad she's dead."

"She's not dead.
She's here.
Down the hall."

I can't control the flood
of tears and rage.
I sob,
shudder,
cry.
I blink.

Dad's gone.
The nurse is doing her midnight check.

Reading

"William?"

I don't recall opening my eyes.
I just suddenly start seeing.

Shasten's standing over me.

I don't recall sleeping,
but I'm just now waking up.

"Hey, you're up."

"Yup."
My voice croaks.

"Don't talk. It's okay.
Just watch this."

Shasten shows me a video
on her phone.

A reporter's talking:

"Two have been killed and two people critically
injured when police responded to a tip at this
Huntington Beach residence."

A uniformed officer's talking:

"We'd been informed that someone had stolen
two firearms, followed by a report of an armed
and dangerous teenaged suspect seen in
this neighborhood."

The reporter:

"What police didn't know was that the teen had
taken these guns to save the lives of two
children ages five and seven from an insidious
abuse ring that's been going on for years."

Pink-Cap teacher:

"The teenager had approached me several
times about his concern for children. I could tell
he was a good kid. I think he's a hero."

I push Shasten's
phone away.

"That's you, William.
That's you they're talking about."

"They don't know
what they're talking about."
I grunt the words.
"Let alone who."

"Well, I think you're a hero.
And Zillah says there's a place for you
at the Institute of Advanced Healing
in Big Sur."

I shake my head,
but it makes me dizzy.
"I can't afford it."

"It's a full scholarship."

"Is that why you're here?
To tell me that?"

> "I'm here because I know you're a good soul.
> And I know my brother's broken collarbone
> wasn't intentional."

"How do you know that?"

> "I can read you now. I saw it."

"Then you know about—"

> "I know Patches survived a terrible childhood."

I start to tell Shasten that it was me,
that there is no kid named Patches,
but she puts her finger to my lips.
Maybe she already knows.

Ollie bursts into the room
carrying a game box.

> "Hey, he's up!
> Welcome back, William.
> Now I can teach you
> all about games."

Behind them, a black spot forms on the ceiling
above their heads.

Dark Thing

A dark thing's been hovering
over my bed for days.
Its shape is feminine,
its eyes crimson.

I receive less medication
because I feel less pain.
The nurse says my head will clear,
but instead the voices are louder.
They call my name,
replay my actions,
and grow blackness in my heart.

The dark thing rains dread and guilt
upon my head.
It drives me from my bed.
But I can only stand for a few minutes
before I'm forced to crawl back
under its crimson-rimmed watch.

I blink and half the day goes by.

     "William? Are you awake?"

I nod.
It's Jill Archer.

     "Feeling any better?"

"Physically, yes,
but otherwise, no,
I'm not."

"I was afraid of that.
Shall we talk about it?"

"Still safe?"

"Yes, I won't tell."

The dark thing over my bed
gurgles.
It shifts its weight as if to listen
to my whispers.

"I'm a murderer."

The dark thing shudders.

"No, William.
Two people died,
but it was self-defense."

"That's how it ended,
but that wasn't my intention."

"What was your intention?"

"To kill my mother
and her husband."

The dark thing shudders again.
My confession strikes at it.

"They raped me,
stole my innocence.

At first I only knew that it hurt.
That it hurt to walk days later.

I only suspected it was wrong,
our 'special secret.'
But I didn't know any better.

There was no one to tell.
Everyone around me seemed in
on my horrible secret.

If Gramps hadn't taken me away,
I don't know
if I would've made it
to my seventh birthday."

          "Your mother sent you away?"

"She didn't know he came to get me.
She'd left me with some guy
in a hotel room.
Gramps never said how he found me."

The dark thing constricts.
Its crimson-rimmed eyes
grow less angry.
Its power over me fades a degree.

"I guess all those years in Kansas
helped me forget what happened."

"It's a common phenomenon
for kids to suppress traumatic events.
Coming back to where it occurred
must have triggered those memories
to resurface."

"And once I did remember,
I went to kill them."

      "But you didn't."

"I didn't know those kids
were there."

      "Your history bred suspicion."

"So I'll get off?"

      "You'll have to pay for the damages
      to your neighbor's house
      and face the burglary charges.
      I think you'll get probation.
      No one wants to prosecute a hero."

The dark thing shrinks
into the corner of the ceiling.

But it's far from gone.

Dead Bird

"William?"

I wake to the sound of my name.
But no one's in my room.

The dark thing above
my bed still watches me
even though it's shrunk.

I have to get out of bed.
Go for a walk.
Escape these walls.

I'm surprised to find a cop
standing right outside my door.

"You need help, son?"

"No."

"Then you've got
to stay
in your room."

Why's a cop standing guard at my door?

The door starts to swing closed,
but I stop it with my foot.

A nurse is rolling a woman
in a wheelchair
down the hallway.
Two police officers escort them.
It's my mother.
In handcuffs.

She's looking down at her hands
with a pained expression,
as if she's holding a dying bird.

She rolls past me
toward the elevator
with her uniformed entourage.

A rush of sorrow
and compassion
rack my body
at the same time.

I don't believe my mother is
completely immoral.
She did step between me
and the bullets.
She did one good act.
Even if all of her previous acts
were monstrous.

I'm sure she'll spin her story
and dance to a tune of her own making
that will offload blame to Alistair.
And that might reduce her sentence.

I don't care.

I'm glad I didn't kill her.
Glad she still lives.
I don't think I could live
with the guilt.

Gramps used to say,
"Taking life,
whether to serve your country
or to protect your loved ones,
leaves a black mark on your soul.
But there's never guilt
when you spare a life."

Killing is wrong.
It's ugly.

I don't think the dark thing
will ever leave me.

Healing

These Zen Griefers
stripped away
my innocence,
my dignity,
and the best parts of
my soul.

I will have to rebuild
a new me.

Therapists can
question me
and offer guidance.

Surgeons can
cut me open
and take out a bullet.

Doctors can
stitch me up
and stop the bleeding.

Nurses can
inject me with medication
and hold back infections.

But all healing
begins deep inside
where unseen scars form.

My first step
is deciding to breathe.
Exhaling the toxic.
Inhaling the invigorating.

My second step
will be learning
to forgive.

I won't forget.
Won't pardon.
I must learn
to coexist with my pain.

I may hate the acts
people have done to me,
but maybe I can
learn to love
their parts that aren't toxic,
learn to love
the things that make a person's character,
in spite of their flaws,
grand.

Maybe I can learn this.
I don't know.

What I do know is that I will survive.
I know that my life still has merit,
even if my past is tainted.

I practice what I've learned from Shasten.
She calls it
a meditation.
Gramps would call it
a prayer.
I would call it
a daily reminder
of how I intend to live
in this world:

Breathe

I let my body fall away.
Allow my mind to clear,
feel my soul rise,
as I fall deeper into my true self.

Breathe

I imagine myself underwater,
being moved by the current,
in a river of honey.

Breathe

I open my mind
to possibilities,
to options,
to dreams.

Breathe

Believe
that I am important,
that I have wisdom,
that I will strive to be kind.

Breathe

I breathe in love,
breathe in hope,
breathe in compassion.

Breathe

I'll seek to
find beauty day to day,
dream of possibilities night after night,
discover wonder moment to moment,
and live in light from breath to breath.

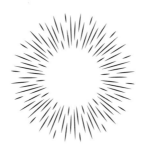

Acknowledgments

Tina Barnett for being my Shasten, showing me the power of compassion, freeing my soul, and for providing me a safe and inspiring space to create.

Charlene Ellen for making me aware.

Jodeen Revere for the River of Honey.

Terri Farley for being my mentor.

Ellen Hopkins for being my role model.

Rana DiOrio for your support and sensitivity.

Emma D. Dryden, without you none of this would have happened. You made Rana aware of me, you were my guide, cheerleader, and navigator through the vast sea of verse. But also you are one of the main reasons why I write YA.

Afterword
by Dr. Donna A. Gaffney, DNSc, PMHCNS-BC, FAAN

There are themes in *Breath to Breath* that startle and shake us to our very core: abandonment, grief and loss, bullying, separation, life transitions, and child sexual abuse. However, embedded in this powerful story is a lesson in triumph. It's not often that we have the opportunity to meet a genuine hero, especially one who is so young. William survives horrors that are not only unspeakable but almost unknowable.

We usually don't "see" the survivors among us. There are no visible signs; they look just like everyone else. They don't talk about the terrible things that caused such pain in their lives. This is true of William.

Prompted by a return to his childhood home, reconnecting with his distant father, and the recent death of his grandfather, William begins to recall and recognize his four-year-old self, a victim of sexual abuse at the hands of his mother and her boyfriend. The fragments of memory come crashing together in the guise of a mysterious and vulnerable little boy named "Patches."

William searches the Internet to learn more about child sexual abuse and assault. He is on the right track; education is a first step to take if you suspect you or a friend has been the victim of sexual abuse or assault. Researchers at the Crimes Against Children Research Center at the University of New Hampshire define child sexual abuse as a range of sexual crimes and offenses perpetrated against children and teens: exhibitionism, pornography, Internet crimes, fondling, and acts that are far more invasive such as oral, anal or vaginal contact. Sexual abuse is usually not a one-time occurrence; it can go on for weeks, months, or years.

In 2014 the Crimes Against Children Research Center analyzed telephone interviews with more than 2000 fifteen-, sixteen-, and seventeen-year-olds and found that one in four girls and one in twenty boys experienced sexual abuse or assault during their lives. The researchers are certain the real numbers may be much higher. Some teens may not remember the abuse and others may be too embarrassed or ashamed to reveal the information.

Most of us have misconceptions about child sexual abuse and the people who perpetrate these terrible crimes. Girls and boys can be sexually abused. We often think that offenders are pedophiles, strangers, or creepy men who lurk in the shadows. They're usually not; the majority of abusers do not fit into these categories. They can be male or female, family members, friends, or acquaintances. And many of these abusers are themselves young people, older children, or teens.

You may be wondering how William could not remember one of the most horrific times in his life. The human brain does some remarkable things to block memories of terrifying incidents. Researchers tell us that traumas like child sexual abuse may not be remembered for years. There can be delayed recall triggered by life changes similar to those experienced by William; the death of a loved one, a move to a new town, a romantic relationship. Sometimes the abuse happens at such a young age that children don't yet have the words to describe or remember it. As these young children grow up they may recollect sensory fragments—the sounds, sights, or even smells of the sexual abuse. Many people will admit such memories are too painful or too confusing and think it may be easiest and best if they suppress or "forget" those memories in order to move on with their lives.

Sexual abuse is surrounded by secrecy, guilt, and shame. These feelings are very commonly experienced and can be so overwhelming that we don't know how to begin the conversation to ask for help. Professionals tell us that if we can talk about our painful experiences our emotional burden will be lighter. Often families and friends are there to listen to us and comfort us. But if the family member or friend is the person who has caused our pain, we pull away and silence ourselves. Not talking about our painful experiences, however, can lead to added difficulties in the years ahead: anxiety, alcohol or substance abuse, troubled relationships, depression, and self-destructive behavior. So the safer someone who's been abused or assaulted can feel about talking with someone they trust, the better.

William is determined to make things better for the people in his life. He's not a bystander. He is an upstander, willing to speak out and take action for others and for himself. Even when the flood of painful emotions threatens a path of hopelessness, William is able to steady himself. The wisdom and support of Gramps and his caring friends bolstered his strength and courage. He knows that this "dark thing will never leave," that he won't forget, but he won't let it define who he is. William knows he will survive.

If you suspect that you or someone you know has been sexually abused or assaulted, reach out to someone you trust. Here are some important things to remember:

• Learn about child sexual abuse and assault.

• Although girls are at greater risk for sexual abuse, boys are also victims.

• Most sexual abuse offenders are known to victims.

• The abuse is not your fault.

• It is never too late to ask for help or support.

The websites below not only provide valuable information on recognizing child sexual abuse; they also offer strategies that reduce the negative consequences of being victimized. You can find out how you can help or get help–for yourself or someone else.

Child Help USA
www.childhelp.org
(For victims and parents)

The National Child Abuse Hotline
1-800-4-A-CHILD (1-800-422-4453)
(For victims and parents)

Crimes Against Children Research Center
University of New Hampshire
www.unh.edu/ccrc
(Excellent resource for professionals)

CyberTipline
www.missingkids.com/cybertipline
(Leads and tips regarding suspected crimes of
sexual exploitation committed against children)

Darkness to Light
www.d2l.org
(Raising awareness about child sexual abuse by
educating adults about the steps they can take)

Male Survivor
www.malesurvivor.org
(Overcoming sexual victimization of boys and men)

National Children's Alliance
www.nationalchildrensalliance.org
(Support, technical assistance, and quality assurance
for child advocacy centers across the country)

National Council on Child Abuse and Family Violence
www.nccafv.org
(A resource center for child abuse prevention, education,
and helplines across the United States)

Rainn

www.rainn.org

(Anti-sexual violence organization; also carries out programs to prevent sexual violence, help victims, and ensure that offenders are brought to justice)

1 in 6

www.1in6.org

(Support for men who have been sexually abused as children)

Dr. Donna Gaffney is a psychotherapist committed to the health and healing of survivors of sexual violence. She is the Advisor for Research and Content Development at the National Alliance for Grieving Children and she consults with children, families, and professionals affected by trauma, loss, and violence. She has counseled young people following individual tragedies and national disasters such as Hurricane Katrina and the terrorist attacks of September 11, 2001, and she coordinated a program for New York health professionals on the evaluation and treatment of sexual assault survivors. Dr. Gaffney holds masters degrees from Teachers College, Columbia University, and Rutgers University, received her doctorate from the University of Pennsylvania, and is the author of The Seasons of Grief, Helping Children Grow Through Loss, *and* Adolescent Sexuality: A Guide for Clinicians.

Letter from William Lewis, the man whose personal journey inspired *Breath to Breath*

Dear Reader,

Early on in the process of healing from my childhood wounds, I decided that I would go through all of this painful work in order to accomplish three things.

The first was to be able to someday be a good parent and husband and to raise my children to be happy and productive adults. I cannot adequately put into words how important that was to me. Having endured such a horrible childhood myself, I felt as though I had to balance the scales by providing my children with an upbringing full of love and support.

The second goal was to help others to heal. I used my gifts of perception to heal myself, and in so doing, I learned a great deal about the processes of healing and recovery. I have applied what I've learned to help others to heal too, but I knew there was another way my journey could serve the cause of healing. I blazed a trail out of the darkness of hatred and pain and into the light of love and forgiveness. I did this so others could more easily find their way out of the dark and into the light. For me, the point of telling my story is to show not only that healing our wounds is possible, but also that it is necessary for our own sake and for the sake of others.

Finally, I wanted to find peace and love within myself and put an end to all the suffering and anguish I lived with every day.

Thank you for taking this journey with me.

William

William Lewis is a healer in the San Francisco Bay Area. He works with individuals and groups remotely and in person to facilitate healing and renewal from a spiritual level. http://www.williamlewishealer.com/

Craig Lew

Craig Lew's storytelling career began even before he learned to write. As a child, he used his father's tape recorder to capture tales about strange planets and scary creatures.

A movie producer, director, award-winning author, illustrator, and screenwriter, Craig still favors a Hitchcockian thriller over a broad teen comedy. Regardless of the genre, he believes the best stories involve a hero who is either seeking love or giving love. At heart he's a big, mushy romantic.

Craig spends his days with his fiancée in a house on a hill with the Corgi land seals Yobo and Zeekie, a three-footed Corgi named Moogie, and Smittens, the kitten with the marshmallow mittens.

Breath to Breath is Craig Lew's first novel for young adults. Learn more about Craig and his work at www.craiglew.com.